My Adventure With
SHEENA
Queen of the Jungle

The Man from Columbia—me.

My Adventure With
SHEENA
Queen of the Jungle
The Making of the Movie *Sheena*

by
Yoram Ben-Ami

BearManor Media

2021

My Adventure With Sheena, Queen of the Jungle:
The Making of the Movie Sheena

© 2021 YODO PRODUCTIONS, LLC

All rights reserved.

All rights reserved. No part of this book may be reproduced or transmitted in any form or by any means, electronic or mechanical, including photocopying, recording, or by any information storage and retrieval system, without permission in writing from the author and appropriate credit to the author and publisher.

Excerpts from non-auctorial interviews and other material appear under a Fair Use Rights claim of U.S. Copyright Law, Title 17, U.S.C. with copyrights reserved by their respective rights holders.

Unless noted otherwise, photographs in this book are from the motion picture *Sheena* ©1984 Colgems Productions Limited, Wiki Commons, or from credited sources. The author has attempted to locate the owner of other photos. Any photographs in question will be removed from future editions upon presentation of proof of ownership by their copyright proprietor.

Comic art for Sheena, Queen of the Jungle is from Wiki Commons

Many of the designations used by manufacturers to distinguish their products are claimed as trademarks or service marks. Where those designations appear in this book and the author and/or publisher was aware of such a claim, the designations contain the symbols ®, ᔆᴹ, or ™. Any omission of these symbols is purely accidental and is not intended as an infringement. Oscar®, Academy Award®, and AMPAS® are registered trademarks of the Academy of Motion Picture Arts and Sciences ©AMPAS.

Published in the United States of America by:

BearManor Media
1317 Edgewater Dr #110
Orlando FL 32804
bearmanormedia.com

Edited by Stone Wallace
Typesetting, cover and layout by John Teehan

Dedication:

With love to Dory Benami
and Nat Segaloff

and to Tanya Roberts—our Sheena—
may she rest in peace

Table of Contents

Author's Preface ix

Do You Speak Swahili? 1

The Kenyan Connection 9

Getting the Green Light 29

Terrific Tanya 43

Ted Wass 49

Flying Wild Animals To Africa 51

Living With Lions 63

Image Secton I 75

Tragedy Strikes 83

Dances With Composers 89

Behind the Camera 99

Image Section II 119

Location, Location, Location 129

Doctor Feelgood 135

Heart Attack In the Jungle 139

Final Shots 143

Appenidx A: A History of Sheena 153

Appenidx B: Film Synopsis 159

Appenidx C: Presskit 165

Index 185

Author's Preface

POOR TANYA ROBERTS. Quite literally the day after I sent the final draft of this book to Ben Ohmart of Bear-Manor Media the news flashed that Tanya, who starred as Sheena, had died. According to first reports—begun by her domestic partner, Lance O'Brien and sadly announced to the media by her representative Mike Pingel—the actress had collapsed on Christmas Eve after returning home from walking her dog and was taken to Cedars-Sinai Hospital where she died.

Within hours, however, further word was released that she was still alive, beginning three days of retractions, corrections, and explanations that were as hopeful as they were confusing. Finally, on January 3, came confirmation that she had, that day, passed away from what was later called a urinary tract infection.

It was a sad, if bizarre, ending for a sweet person and a devoted actress with whom I very much had enjoyed working years ago when we were both young and fearless and finding our way in Africa for Columbia Pictures.

I hope that this book is a fitting tribute to Tanya, just as I hope it is to the hundreds of people, both behind the scenes and in front of the cameras, who worked terribly hard under unforgiving conditions to make what we hoped would be an entertaining movie.

The movie *Sheena, Queen of the Jungle* could not be made today. Nor should it be made. But it was, back in 1984, and that's what this book is about.

Much, but not enough, has changed since then. What was accepted (or at least tolerated) in 1984 is now rightly damned. The overt racism of Jim Crow, if not the institutionalized racism in American DNA, was felt but largely unspoken at the time cameras rolled on what was dismissed as a "female Tarzan" movie. Indeed, although Edgar Rice Burroughs' Tarzan, introduced in 1912, drew criticism for its stereotypes of Africans, Sheena, who debuted in comics in 1937, seems to have dodged many similar attacks, perhaps because they were superseded by criticism of her sexuality.

Both Tarzan and Sheena promote what Rudyard Kipling condescendingly called the "White Man's Burden," and I wish we had made criticism of it an element in *Sheena*. But we didn't know to.

We also weren't making satire (although some critics said we did, albeit accidentally). We were just making an adventure film that overcame production obstacles that no previous Hollywood movie had ever faced.

My Adventure with Sheena arrives now as the Black Lives Matter movement challenges the conscience of the country as no crusade has achieved since the Civil Rights Struggle of the 1950s. It also follows the uplifting 2008 election of Barack Obama (whose father was Kenyan) as President and the 2020 election of Kamala Harris (whose father is Jamaican) as Vice President. My hope as the author of this book and the executive producer of the film is to use reminiscences of *Sheena* to contrast how society was at the time it was made, how society has changed since, and to urge for this change to continue.

The now-outdated, even offensive, ideas behind *Sheena* were not intended as malice; they were the conventions of the time. Most of our African cast and crew members realized this. Good and fair people have evolved since then, but it's helpful to look to the past for clues of how far we still need to go. It's in the spirit of growth, progress, and unity that I'm writing about *Sheena*.

That was then, this is now.

Do You Speak Swahili?

SUDDENLY THERE SHE WAS. A woman, blond as the sun, walking toward me. She wore nothing but a leather bikini. I was in the office of Guy McElwaine, the head of Columbia Pictures, and I was waiting for her with Guy and director John Guillermin. There was a woman walking with her: Ann Roth, the award-winning costume designer. As she walked past other people on the studio lot, she turned heads but returned none of their glances. A few moments later there was a knock on the door and Tanya Roberts—that was her name, the star of *Charlie's Angels* (and would soon star in the next James bond film)—walked in. She was sexy and knew she was; she owned the room the moment she entered it. This was the first time I met *Sheena, Queen of the Jungle*. It was a wardrobe-fitting meeting to approve what she would be wearing every day for months in the African sun. It was made of brown leather—a minimum of leather—and showed off her perfectly sculpted figure.

It would be my job to produce the movie, and I didn't have to wear a bikini to do it.

My adventure started at the end of June 1983. My agent, Sam Schwartz, picked me up and drove me to our lunch with Columbia Pictures production executive Sheldon "Shel" Schrager. Two things were already unusual: first, that my agent picked me up instead of telling me to meet him at the studio. Second, the fact that Sam Schwartz represented me at all. I was a producer and Sam specialized in big-name composers such as John Williams, Randy Newman, James Horner, and Ennio Morricone. Schwartz had a score in mind for me, but it wasn't the musical kind.

"Do you speak any Swahili?" he asked as I got in the car.

"What the hell do I know about Swahili?" I said. "I can barely speak English." This was not completely true; I had lived in America since 1979 and had been making pictures with a pretty good grasp of the language, but I was born in Israel and my first language was Hebrew.

"Never mind," Sam prompted me. "When they ask, say that you can. And how well do you know Africa?"

"Never set foot there," I said.

"Also keep that between us."

The affable Shel Schrager was Vice President of Production at Columbia under company President of Production John Veitch. For several years, the studio had been trying to develop a feature film of the *Sheena, Queen of the Jungle* comic book created by Will Eisner and Jerry Iger in 1937. The script was written by David Newman and Leslie Stevens, depicting a white girl whose parents were killed in an African country. She is raised by an African Shaman who becomes her surrogate mother, teaching her to communicate with the animals. When a corrupt local ruler seeks to exploit the country's natural resources for his own ends, Sheena, working with an American sports broadcaster with whom she has a chaste romance, rallies her animal friends to set things right.

None of anybody's attempts had come to fruition and Columbia was about to write it off as a bad investment, but not before making one last attempt. Somehow they had found a way to give Sheena another life, and Sam Schwartz knew it, and it was his scheme to propose me as the solution to their *Sheena* production problems.

"Columbia is in trouble," he began. "They committed to make *Sheena*. They have a big-time director signed to do it. They have a script. Now they have Tanya Roberts as Sheena. But they need somebody to control all these elements, especially the headstrong director John Guillermin."

"Columbia's been making movies for sixty years," I said, shaking my head in astonishment. Something didn't make sense. "What's different about this one?"

"First," Sam said, "they want to shoot it in Africa but they're not sure if it can be done because no major American film company has made a whole movie in Africa lately. Second," he said, getting on the 101 freeway to Burbank, "this thing has been rattling around their studio for seven or eight years. At one time they wanted to shoot it in South America, at another time in Mexico, and most recently on the back lot."

"A jungle picture on the back lot?" I said.

"The director said he'd walk if they tried that. He's a strong director. Uncontrollable. He'll eat you alive. He even has a business partner who he wants to be the co-producer. Watch yourself."

This struck me as odd. "It's strange that, after looking in all the wrong places, the studio now actually wants to shoot the picture in Africa."

"In Kenya," Sam said.

"What changed their mind?"

Sam smiled the kind of smile an agent smiles when the conversation turns to money. "Columbia was bought last year by the Coca-Cola Company and became a subsidiary," he started. "Coca-Cola has bottling plants all over the world, including East Africa, which is Kenya." He leaned closer. "Do you know what frozen assets are?"

"Sure," I said. "They're profits a company makes in a foreign country but the country won't allow them to take out because it might collapse their economy."

"Exactly," Sam said. "Columbia—which is to say Coca-Cola—has millions of dollars trapped in Kenya and the only choice they have is to make the movie there, to pay for it in Kenyan shillings, and to be credited in dollars in America for this expense and investment at Coca-Cola headquarters in Atlanta."

"But why do they want me out of everybody else in town?"

"Because you're a troubleshooter, Yoram. You're somebody who can go into the field and solve problems that come up. You're Israeli, they'll probably look at you like you were in the Mossad and can handle any kind of operation anywhere in the world. On top of that, you brought in your last picture ahead of schedule and under budget."

He was referring to *Lone Wolf McQuade*, starring Chuck Norris, David Carradine, and Barbara Carrera. Orion Pictures gave us $4.5 million to make the picture and, working closely with director Steve Carver, we not only wrapped early, we returned $250,000 to Orion Pictures in unspent funds and opened the picture as the number one box office attraction in America. In Hollywood terms, this made me a hot property.

Sam didn't stop. "These guys don't know the first thing about shooting a whole film in Africa. No studio has done it in decades. They don't want it to be a National Geographic nature special. They want it to be a big-time summer release that will play in thousands of theatres. You've pulled together shoots that should never have happened," he continued. "It's your time, Yoram. Strike while the iron is hot, because it won't last forever." He looked at me to drive home his point.

"By the way," he said, as we pulled into the studio gate, "you never told me if you knew how to speak Swahili?"

"Not a word," I said.

Sam turned to me and smiled slyly. "From now on you do. As long as they don't, they'll never know. And tell them that you know Africa very well."

Columbia's offices were in The Burbank Studio on Alameda Avenue in Burbank. We met Shel Schrager in the studio commissary and went directly into the Executive Dining Room. Unlike the dining area for below-the-line personnel, which was a sea of Formica-topped tables, the Executive Dining Room featured table linen, silver cutlery, and attentive servers. The food could rival any fine restaurant. We had a cordial meal, exchanged typical Hollywood talk about people we knew in common, what pictures we'd liked lately, and who in town was about to be hired or fired (present company excluded). Shel confirmed what I had suspected: the studio was almost committed to *Sheena* but didn't know how to move forward. Shel, who had worked his way up from assistant director to production VP, knew filmmaking inside out. He stressed to me that they needed a watchdog producer to keep director John Guillermin in line.

Shel signed for the meal (which I expected to be charged to the budget of somebody's picture, probably mine) and we went off to the big meeting with his boss, head of production John Veitch.

In Veitch's fancy office I was introduced to members of Columbia's production team. Everyone was sitting comfortably on couches. They were all staring at me. Although I was going there for a job interview, I felt more like a gladiator entering the Coliseum. Then I met the director.

John Guillermin sat almost rebelliously on his couch, away from the others, so he could take it all in. He was tan, trim, and looking, although fifty-eight, no more than his middle forties. Even sitting silently, he threw off an air of self-assurance, exactly the aura that drives fear into the hearts of already-fearful studio executives. It can also make him an enemy to a producer, so I instinctively went on my guard. Making matters even more complicated was the fact that Guillermin was a former client of Guy McElwaine, who now ran the studio and was undoubtedly responsible for hiring him. (Welcome to Hollywood!)

The interview started. I knew I was in over my head. I hadn't been in Africa. I didn't speak Swahili. I was standing before people who had experience in huge numbers of big-budget movies. At some point I said to myself, "Fuck it, I don't have a chance in hell of getting this job, so I'll just be myself and say whatever I want. I'll just be me."

"Can I get you something to drink?" John Veitch asked.

"Thank you," I said nonchalantly. "I'll have a Diet Pepsi."

It just came out. The room fell silent. Even the birds outside stopped chirping. It was as if I had said I'd slept with the Columbia lady. Then it hit me: I had just asked the top people who worked for Coca-Cola for a drink from their biggest rival. Fortunately, I'm good at thinking on my feet and making the best out of bad situations.

"Diet Pepsi?" Veitch said surprisedly, astonished that I had said such a thing in the Temple of Coca-Cola. "I don't think you want to get this job." "No, I do," I said, and started to laugh. Most importantly, John Guillermin also started to laugh. It was the kind of laugh that said, "This guy has balls." Once he laughed, everybody else did. They all thought I purposely said it as a joke.

That's when I knew I had the job. After that, they didn't ask me a single question relating to the picture. (John Guillermin told me later that my performance in this meeting assured him that he could bond with me and that I didn't lose my presence of mind in tough situations.)

After that, Sam Schwartz went to work on my contract. I was to get a hefty fee for that time, plus a *per diem* (daily expenses on top of salary) for my personal use, and all other expenses paid. I was offered the title of Executive Producer.

Only one obstacle stood in our way: Africa. We had to go there to find locations and make contact with the Kenyan government officials whose cooperation was essential. This was easier said than done; the president of Kenya, Daniel arap Moi, had barely survived a recent coup attempt and was skeptical of meeting new people. Rebels were believed to be reassembling in neighboring Somalia. Worse, Kenya didn't have an experienced film commissioner; everything was handled directly out of the President's office.

Frank Price, the head of Columbia, laid down the law: before the company finally decides whether to make *Sheena*, go to Kenya and determine whether it is rational and safe to shoot there. Guillermin and I were handed our marching orders and sent off together on a "recce" (pronounced "reckie"), which is slang for a reconnaissance mission that includes a location scout. A few days later, as I packed my bag, I felt like Stanley embarking to find Livingston. I kissed my wife, Ani, goodbye for now, hugged my eight-year-old son Dory, assured him that Abba (Hebrew for Daddy) would be back, and set my jaw for whatever happened.

Having never been to Africa, my mind filled with wild fantasies. Would we be welcomed in Kenya? Would I be cooked in a kettle by cannibals (like I used to see in the old movies)? Would lions surround the plane when we landed?

As they say in Swahili, *chochote kinaweza kutokea* (anything can happen).

The Kenyan Connection

JOHN GUILLERMIN WAS FORMIDABLE. At fifty-eight, he was an accomplished filmmaker of such large-canvas productions as *The Bridge at Remagen*, (1969), *The Towering Inferno* (1974), and the remake of *King Kong* (1975), as well as earlier, more intimate features: *I Was Monty's Double* (1958), *Waltz of the Toreadors* (1962) and *Guns at Batasi* (1964). Educated at the City of London School and Cambridge University, he joined the RAF as World War II was winding down. He began shooting documentaries at age 22. He and a business partner formed their own production company in England in 1948 and turned out a few small features before Guillermin set out for Hollywood two years later to conquer the studios. He was a journeyman director until 20th Century-Fox production chief Darryl F. Zanuck took a liking to him and graced him with a succession of larger and larger pictures culminating with *The Blue Max* (1966), starring George Peppard as a World War I German flying ace thirsting after his country's top military medal.

Like Peppard's ace, Guillermin, too, sought recognition. Although his films range from the romantic crime drama

PJ (1978) to the western *El Condor* (1970), he was most at home commanding large crews and logistically complex projects. This made him perfect for *Sheena.*

John was considered argumentative, stubborn, and manipulative. But he was also knowledgeable, unflappable, and decisive (except, surprisingly, on our flight to Kenya during which he irritated the First Class cabin attendants by first wanting, then not wanting, and finally wanting his meal). This was the first example I saw of a condition I came to call the "love-to-fuck-with-you" syndrome. For example, one morning during the shoot we were waiting at the hotel to be picked up by our car to be taken to location, As we stood there, Susi Olroyd, the script supervisor, joined us to go to the set and said casually, "Good morning, Yoram," and then, to John, gave a pleasant, "Did you sleep well, John?"

John took a pause and then shot back at her, "What the fuck do you care how I slept?" Out of the blue, that's what he said to her. It was so harsh and for no reason that she went back inside the hotel with tears in her eyes. To make it worse, after that she had to be at his side all day long for months taking continuity notes. Despite this, he always got the best crews to work with him on his pictures. That was John.

John had the personality of a commander, not only in his ability to get the job done but not caring who he stepped on to do it. Producer David L. Wolper said he was "a pain in the ass" who nearly caused the crew of *The Bridge at Remagen* to quit *en masse.*[1] Norma Barzman, the widow of *Blue*

---
1. Wolper, David. *Producer: A Memoir.* New York: Scribner, 2003.

Max co-writer Ben Barzman, wrote of him as being difficult with a "cold, stiff-lipped manner,"[2] an opinion shared by the film's producer, Elmo Williams, who called him "demanding [and] indifferent to people getting hurt as long as he got realistic action" whom "the crew disliked."[3] Novelist James Dickey (*Deliverance*) called him a megalomaniac after their project, *Alnilam*, fell apart. Even the normally diplomatic Charlton Heston (*Skyjacked*, 1972) admitted that he had an "irascible streak." John also had a habit of being fired, most notably from the big-budget films *Midway* (1976, replaced by Jack Smight) and *Sahara* (1973, replaced by Andrew V. McLaglen).

He was certainly impressive. Athletic, in impeccable shape, with angular features, a full head of brown hair swept back over a tall forehead, and with a patrician bearing, he carried himself in the manner of a British colonial lord. As with many men who survived World War II, particularly those in the elite flying corps, no situation fazed him and he was intimidated by no living creature. That invulnerability was to be tragically tested during the making of *Sheena* but that was yet to come.

As we flew first class to Kenya on our mission to see if we could get the job done, I knew I was at a disadvantage. John had already shot two films there: *Tarzan's Greatest Adventure* (1959) and *Shaft in Africa* (1973). Truth be told, only the exteriors of *Tarzan* had been filmed in Kikuyu land, Kenya with interiors completed at Pinewood Studios

---

2. Barzman, Norma. *The Red and the Blacklist: The Intimate Memoir of a Hollywood Expatriate.* New York: Thunder's Mouth Press, 2003.
3. Williams, Elmo. *Elmo Williams: A Hollywood Memoir.* Jefferson, NC: McFarland and Company, 2006.

in England, and *Shaft in Africa* took place in New York, Paris, and Spain as well as Addis Ababa, Ethiopia and Massawa, Eritrea. By that measure, *Sheena* would be the first American studio film to be made entirely in Kenya, and he would be in charge of doing it.

John relished the idea. He had fought the studio to do it his way, telling them, "If you want someone to shoot it in Mexico, South America, or California, get somebody else. I was in Africa. Africa looks different from Mexico or a set." They caved. And yet I also realized that, even though John's and my goal would be making the movie, the studio's and Coca-Cola's goal was to use their frozen assets.[4] It was like two buses heading in the same direction but on different routes. I also knew that a director of John's imagination would add touches to the screenplay when he set up the scenes—expensive touches that would drive up the budget.

A lot had changed in Kenya since John had last been there a quarter century earlier. When he shot *Tarzan's Greatest Adventure* in 1958, the country was in the twilight of British colonial rule. The Mau-Mau Rebellion (1952-1959) had shaken the Crown's grip on the volatile nation and the Kenya National African Union was poised to take over. Which is not to say that Kenya was becoming politically stable. The years after its official independence in 1964 saw repeated attempts to topple President Jomo Kenyatta,

---

4. Frozen assets, sometimes called "blocked funds," became a financing issue in the 1950s as studios found that their foreign income was being impounded in countries like Kenya, India, Spain, Yugoslavia and other tenuous economies. The only way to turn receipts into cash was to shoot all or part of a film there. When multi-national corporations began buying old-line Hollywood studios in the 1960s and 70s this became an even greater factor as not only movie revenues but all corporate revenues in such countries were being frozen. It also explains why some films of the era (*Willie and Phil, Close Encounters of the Third Kind*, etc.) suddenly went to India and other locales.

and uprisings continued to assail President Daniel arap Moi when he succeeded Kenyatta in 1978. As I would learn, there were two governments in Kenya: the one that ran the country and the one that ran the government.

John and I were going alone. Later, if Columbia decided to green-light the film, we would return for another recce, at that time with a creative team. In a goodbye phone call, my agent Sam Schwartz said to me, "Be careful of the alligator." I said, "What do you mean?" Sam said, "Be careful of Guillermin." I told him I would.

What I did not know at the time was that Guillermin's participation ultimately depended upon his finding just the right locations to bring his vision to the screen. While I was auditioning John, John was auditioning Africa.

We landed at Nairobi's Embakasi International Airport (now called the Jomo Kenyatta International Airport) where, much to my relief, our plane was not met by lions. Instead, we were met by a driver for Coca-Cola East Africa who took us, not to the hotel, but to meet Pierre Ferrari, the company's head of marketing for the region. As with people who, after a while, look like their dogs, Ferrari looked like a Coke bottle. He was an interesting man. He had started with the company's wine business in the early 70s and rose through successive positions to the point at which we met. (He would later become senior vice president of marketing for Coca-Cola U.S.A.). He received us cordially and we discussed the mountains of Kenyan shillings gathering dust that *Sheena* was designed to liberate from local banks. I also stressed the most important thing, which was finding out if it was safe to shoot in his politically unstable country.

"We need government assistance and security protection," I said.

"I think it's safe," Ferrari said, "but, if you want, I can check." He picked up the phone and spoke a few short instructions in Swahili. Shortly he hung up and told me, "I can arrange a meeting with President Daniel arap Moi. He is interested in reestablishing tourism and wants to prove that his country is safe and that you can shoot quietly, with all the necessary assistance. Let me know." Having said that, the meeting was over and John and I proceeded to the hotel.

Nairobi, Kenya's Norfolk Hotel is a two-story Tudor-style structure that opened its doors on Christmas day, 1904, and has been one of the world's great hotels ever since. Its 170 rooms (many of which are spacious bungalows) and four restaurants make an imposing fortress. When I stayed there for *Sheena*, it was owned by a Jewish family, the Blocks (it is now part of the Fairmont chain), who had acquired it in 1972. On New Year's Eve, 1980, a bomb planted there by an Arab terrorist exploded, killing several people and doing extensive damage. In repairing the building, Block took the opportunity to add a restaurant, ballroom, and a pair of function rooms that had been in operation for a year by the time we arrived. (After we left it was used in the film *Out of Africa*, 1985.) Its style may be Tudor, but its history is colonial; it was built by the British—a huge stone structure with polished wooden floors and rich, wood-covered walls, and a garden stocked with local animals and birds. But before reaching the registration desk, you walk through a huge terrace that, no matter what time of day, you see a cast of European tourists enjoying the air, being waited on by tuxedo-clad servers. On closer inspection you begin to notice that they look more like a group of international spies. I stopped to take it all in, seeing the hotel and the terrace and the people, and felt like I was in a scene from the movie *Casablanca*.

As I stopped, I heard my name. "Yoram!" I was shocked. Who knows me here? I walked toward the voice and "Mr. X" stood up with a glass of whiskey in his hand, smiled at me, and invited me to sit with him at his table. Even after so many years I still have to call him "Mr. X" because I don't want to endanger his life. He was an international arms dealer that worked in Africa and looked exactly like what I described when I saw the crowd there. We had mutual friends in Israel when I used to live there, but I did not expect to meet him here. We spoke in Hebrew.

"What brings a clown like you here, or do I have to ask what you've decided to do with your life?"" he said.

"Well, it's my first time in Africa. I am now a film producer in Hollywood and I need help."

"What kind of help?"

I explained to him that Columbia Pictures is interested in making a huge movie to be shot completely in Kenya, but I understand that the political situation here is very tense. We have to get assurances that the movie would be supported and completed with the help of the Kenyan military and government. I need to get to the top, to the President, and find if it's safe to bring two hundred foreigners, equipment, and millions of dollars here.

"Mr. X" lit his cigarette and said, " "No problem. I can arrange a meeting for you with the President and you will get what you need."

Oh great, I thought, another arrogant Israeli who brags that he can do things nobody else can do. Then he leaned closer to me and confided, "Let me tell you something. Last night, on the border with Somalia, terrorists murdered two Germans on a tourist bus. That's a news item that won't be published here for several days, but you know it from me now."

I thanked him and went to my suite where I unpacked and made myself comfortable. Then I phoned Ferrari and asked, as casually as I could, if he had heard anything about a terrorist attack on the Somali border. He had not. This made it clear to me that he was a nice man but not in the loop, so to speak. In other words, I could not depend on his assurances.

Later, John and I went to dinner. Throughout our dinner, I felt that he was feeling me out to see if I was the enemy or if he could bring me into his camp. We were like two dogs sniffing each other's asses.

In theory, a producer's job is to do everything possible to help the director make the movie. In practice, the producer and director are sometimes not making the same movie, and it's essential to iron out any differences before the shoot starts. Knowing that John was headstrong, I wanted to give him complete support without becoming his patsy; likewise, knowing I was the studio's representative, John surely did not want to make me an enemy.

John was smart; he had great instincts; he was a survivor. We started to talk about the script (which was still being tweaked by Lorenzo Semple, Jr. who had been John's writer on *King Kong*) before going on recce the next day. As two men will do, we shared war stories and then got down to how he was going to shoot an important scene: the assassination of the King by minions of his brother. To this day, I remember the way he described how he was planning to stage it: standing up, he grabbed a pretend spear and acted it out just as he would direct the performer to do. "He takes the spear," he said with the loud voice of a radio announcer, "and throws it with all his might. It passes through a glass window, shattering it into pieces, and heads straight on to pierce the heart of the king!"

Watching him, feeling his enthusiasm, and knowing the script, I could actually see it happening in front of my eyes. It was so powerful that I thought to myself, "I am so happy to be in this business, getting to work with directors like John." Of course, I knew I was being manipulated. He manipulated everybody. But I was manipulating him, too.

That night, too keyed up to go to sleep, I took a taxi from the hotel and asked the Kenyan driver to take me to a club that's friendly to tourists. I still didn't speak Swahili, but he knew just enough English to speed me to Florida 2000.

Florida 2000 was a disco that was a hangout for anybody who wanted anything. It was full of black women on the lookout for *mzungu*, the Swahili name for white men. At the time, mzungus looked down at black Africans, and the women who stationed themselves throughout Florida 2000 tolerated it because they believed that all white men had money. This was made clear to me when I entered and walked up rickety wooden stairs to the second-floor bar. Along the way, woman after woman stood there with her hand out begging for pennies, cigarettes, and paper money. That was with one hand. With their other hand they groped my groin freely and shamelessly. I never felt more "popular" in my life.

I started a conversation with a bald, plump German sailor named Stefan who explained, when a young woman stepped between us and pushed her chest into mine, "She'll have rum or whiskey or whatever, and you'll be happy to smoke a cigarette." Then he signaled to one of the vacant wooden chairs. "You're a *mzungu*. They'll do anything for you, no matter what you look like. They're whores, of course." He pointed to one he said was named Josephine and said, "They finished me, I just got to drink tonight." I had no interest in either Stefan or Josephine, but when you buy a drink for a stranger you're actually paying a listener fee, so I had no choice but to hear his story for a few shillings. By two A.M. the jet lag caught up with me and I went alone back to the hotel.

The next morning I had a formal meeting with an attaché at the American Embassy in Nairobi who was a black African-American. He was friendly and efficient and he said, "You're representing Coca-Cola and Columbia Pictures, two big American corporations, and I am ready to call the President's office."

I smiled to him and said, "Thank you very much for your offer but I have a problem."

"What do you mean?"

"I don't know whose help I should choose. I have three people. One is Your Excellency, the other one is Pierre Ferrari from Coca-Cola Africa, and the third one is a guy by the name of… (I told him "Mr. X"'s real name)… who are ready to help me. Who should I go with?" I asked.

The attaché smiled and, to my surprise, said, "Go with "Mr. X," the Israeli guy." To make his point, he held up both index fingers and pushed them together to demonstrate how close "Mr. X" was with the President's office. "But if you need any additional help, ask me."

I went back to "Mr. X" who agreed to make the connection. Then he told me something that you wouldn't expect to hear from an arms dealer, but that has guided my business and personal relationships ever since. "You're in their country," he said of the Kenyans. "First thing, they are as civilized as we are and should be treated as such. If it helps you get used to it, always think of them as if they are a white man. Second, they are smart, so don't think you can fool them. And third, they work mainly through personal connections. The President will help you because of me, not because you're bringing money to the country or are helping the economy. If you make any problems, then my ass goes, and my connections are ruined. I can afford to help you on condition only that my connections are not harmed."

I told him, "I would really appreciate it if you would help us out so I could go back to Los Angeles and tell the studio we can shoot this movie here in Kenya."

Like almost every Israeli, he said again, "Don't worry" and then said, "Now go back to Hollywood and tell them everything is safe and will be fine."

With that confidence in my mind, I went out with Guillermin on our first recce. In searching for locations where he would shoot the script, John did not seem to know what distance was. He insisted on locations that were so far apart from each other that traveling the crew between them would be a major logistical task. The more time I spent with him, the more I saw that he was in his element. A trim and wildly energetic man, he loved going around shirtless, drinking in the hot July sun, excited at the prospect of filming against the beautiful African landscapes. We were different. I had grown up on a kibbutz in Israel and I'd had my fill of working in the hot sun. I was happy when he finally retired to his bungalow.

On the night of July 22nd, which happened to be my fortieth birthday, I waited until John had gone to sleep. I took a shower, dressed in a full suit and tie, and, at 11 o'clock, went to have dinner at the hotel. The kitchen was still open, but I found myself alone in the huge, luxurious dining room. Liveried waiters stood all around me, each tasked with a separate job: fill the water glass, serve dishes, clear dishes, brush the table, etc. I missed my wife Ani and my son Dory. I thought, Here I was, producing a movie for a major Hollywood studio, the pinnacle of my career as a filmmaker, a man who came from nowhere in Israel and is now an Executive Producer. "How did I get here?" I wondered. "In my profession I have met and worked with movie stars and incredibly talented individuals, artists that most people around the world will only see on the screen if they buy a ticket. Here I am getting paid to watch people like Tanya Roberts in a bikini…"

My thoughts took me back to Israel, where I was born into a family that gave up on me practically from the start.

The worst thing that can happen to a baby is to have a mother like I had. From the first moment that I came out of her belly, there were tons of expectations put on my shoulders. Life had become a clash between the chances that I have and the various expectations, some of them strange, of my father and my mother. I was asked as a kid to fill all her dreams myself and I failed again and again and again. At the end of the day, I was considered as a black sheep, a bad kid, untalented, and a loss.

We lived in a very small town in the British Mandate of Palestine years before it would become the State of Israel. It had a Hebrew name: Ness Ziona. We were a small community surrounded by Arab villages. There were no streets and we had a lot of English soldiers driving back and forth patrolling in commando Jeeps. People in Ness Ziona didn't have any money, and my family had less than everybody. We were just another family of laborers for whom work was the center of their being. We would be defined today as a very low-income family, but my parents were Pioneers, the generation that built the State of Israel. They came from Romania to create the Zionist dream.

Our life was concentrated in Ness Ziona and I, the little kid, was supposed to find my own way to grow up. There was nothing to eat at home; we just bought food for the next day. Despite this, when I was four years old, my mother sent me to study how to play the violin. This was only because Mordechai, the son of our neighbors, who was three years older than I was, was doing it. My mother always wanted her son to be like Mordechai. After the second lesson, which was very costly, the violin teacher told my mother that I will not be Jascha Heifetz. At that time, they didn't know how to define ADHD or OCD.[5] Nevertheless, I ended up working in communications and entertainment, which require listening and concentration. Years later I said to my Beverly Hills shrink, "Couldn't you have told me this fifty years ago? Where were you when I was four years old?"

Only then did I realize that, all my life, I loved facing challenges. When I was young I was constantly told "you cannot do this" and "you cannot do that" and, in effect, to hide in the corner and not try for the center. That became my Life's challenge: to go for the center in everything I did. But the trouble was that once I got to the center I became less interested in the challenges that got me there. I have found that there are many people like me who were told that they cannot overcome problems. I got to the stage where this really intrigued me; if, for example, you told me not to move the mountain, I would see it as a challenge and would try to move it.

It was many years before I learned that about myself. As a child, those were the days when parents would beat you if you failed at something. Mine did—with a belt—because I was not like Mordechai who took violin. On top of that, when I was six and went to elementary school, Mordechai became my teacher in Math and English. I told my Beverly Hills shrink about that, too.

If a kid is lucky he has a role model such as a teacher or a father. Mordechai became my sort-of idol. Because of him, I had a chance to see other heroes that I wanted to be like. I met them at the movies. Here is how it happened.

---

5. Attention Deficit Hyperactivity Disorder and Obsessive-Compulsive Disorder.

Mordechai was very good with English and had a job at the local Ness Ziona theatre running the subtitle machine for non-Hebrew language films. Back then the subtitles were on a separate strip of film that had to be projected on the screen at the side of the picture. You changed the subtitles by pulling on a rope that scrolled the Hebrew words. Mordechai's job was to sit in the back of the theatre with the machine, follow the dialogue, and change the subtitles.

One afternoon Mordechai got me out of school and we went to the movies. The theatre was almost empty because who could afford to buy a ticket? Mordechai loved to eat, and that day there was a small audience and he wanted to go to the concession stand to buy a sandwich. I begged him to let me work the subtitle machine while he was gone. "What do I do?" I asked.

"Just watch the picture and keep up with the dialogue."

Unfortunately, I didn't understand enough English to keep in sync with what the actors were saying and I finished ten minutes ahead of the movie.

When I wasn't messing up subtitles, I was watching the movies even before I knew how to understand their English. Like children all over the world, I loved Hollywood movies and fell in love with Errol Flynn, John Wayne, Clark Gable, Burt Lancaster, and Gregory Peck. Those became my role models. Every movie that I saw, afterward, as I walked out onto the empty streets, I acted like the hero I had just seen. If it was a John Wayne movie, I would strut down the street expecting a showdown at high noon. If it was Gregory Peck, I wanted to be a lawyer arguing a case. If I saw *Gone with the Wind* I tried to imitate Clark Gable.

Life was different then; you couldn't aspire to be anything. People from small places like ours weren't supposed to have dreams. I was like the little boy in *Cinema Paradiso* who one day realizes that he has to leave town if he wants to fulfill his yearning for movies.

There was one dramatic event that changed my life. On one of those very hot days I went to the outside market, like a swap meet, with my mother. I was three or four years old and my mother was carrying me. Because of the heat, she didn't mind that I got down and walked behind her. I didn't see it coming but I went to the main road and it was a Jeep with soldiers that came towards me. There was no road and behind them was a lot of dust. I ran towards the Jeep and my mother, at the last moment, saw me and ran. She managed to push me away but she fell under the Jeep and was thrown about ten feet in the air. The price was three months in the hospital and limping for the rest of her life. I was the guilty one, the "accused." She and other people held me responsible. My mother loved me until the accident, but afterward I went from being a prince to an ugly duckling that ruined his mother's life. How can you expect to teach or to educate a kid after a trauma like this, especially when people come to you every day and tell you, "Oh how beautiful your mother was before the accident." There was not a single day that I didn't feel that I owed my life to my mother. It was made clear to me that I was not the most talented kid in the world, and it was also made clear to me that my mother was no longer the most beautiful woman in the world. It was all my fault.

My father was a *schmatte*, a rag. My mother ran the house with total control. He couldn't stand against her. She married him because he was good-looking. They were thirty years old when they got married. A typical scene when I was ten years old: my father, who was a brick layer, comes back from a very hot working day, tired, sweating, and my mother is waiting to tell him what a bad kid I was during the day. She told him everything about the troubles and the tsuris that I made for her during the day and he would beat me. And yet after that, when I went to bed, my father would quietly open the bedroom door and enter. Assuming I was asleep, he would walk over to my bed and give me a kiss on my forehead. He didn't know that I was pretending to be asleep, like an actor, because I loved his kisses. I still remember them all these years later. This is how I became an actor.

He loved me but had no hopes for me. He thought I might be like him, a simple bricklayer. He told me, "I don't see that you are going to have a glimmering future. You probably will end up being a truck driver. You should marry a hairstylist or somebody who can help you support your family when you grow up." Nothing like being ten years old and getting that kind of pep talk.

All of these memories sifted through my mind as I sat alone in the Norfolk Hotel dining room having dinner. I was happy to be there by myself without Guillermin who—with his erudition, education, and manner—always had to be the center of attention. I was alone, but I wasn't lonely.

Across the dining room an impeccably dressed older black Kenyan pianist serenaded his sole listener (me) with expertly played music. In his appearance and manner, he perfectly matched the elegance of the room. Moreover, he seemed to know selections from every country and every musical era that had arrived to Africa, recent hits as well as standards. He was a good player but, as I started my dinner, I was afraid that he would go on a break before I finished. I got up, walked to him, and—feeling the ambiance mood of the hotel—said, like Humphrey Bogart, "You played it for her, you can play it for me. If she can stand it, I can. Play it." Then I handed him a $100 bill. This was a lot of money for him He laughed, knew what I was quoting, and stayed at the keyboard till two in the morning playing "As Time Goes By." If you must have a birthday dinner alone, this was the way to do it.

The morning after my birthday a tall, elegant man was waiting outside for John and me. This was Tor Allen who, with his wife, Sue, operated the finest safari enterprise in Kenya (he would later work with us on our film). Naturally he wore the traditional khaki safari outfit, but that was the only traditional thing about him. Instead of going on a simple sightseeing trip, Tor's customers traveled in style; following their Land Rover, which Tor himself drove, was another vehicle laden with large tents, soft beds, protective netting, comfort facilities, and a complete kitchen unit (because you can't eat sandwiches for three days). Tor would be taking John and me on a grueling motor trek through Kenya's natural wonders, both geological and zoological. I was looking forward to it, not only for the wonders we would see but for the opportunity to further bond with John. Although we weren't going as tourists, Tor gave us a checklist to mark the animals we saw as well as lending us his expertise by leading us to locations for John to consider in making the film.

I will never forget his promise to take us to places that "no other white person had been to." This was important; Guillermin, like other directors, didn't like to film where other directors had already shot. This began a journey into areas I never thought I would ever see. Wild—very wild—animals came up to the Land Rover, touched it, tested us, and kept going—except for the time that two huge elephants rushed us from the brush, trumpeting their annoyance. As Tor threw our vehicle into gear, I knew why the Land Rover had earned its reputation as the number one car to have with you on safari. We continued our location search, driving across rivers and between trees, dodging animals, and then came to the end of what passed for a road. And what do I see there? An old metal sign saying "Coca-Cola." No white men, indeed! It was probably left over from the time of the colonial Brits.

The total "Tor experience" was great. I liked him and, more importantly, John liked him. As a result I made him the Safari Director on the picture.

As for John, he fell in love with Africa, as I did. He was fully aboard. On October 10, 1983 I telexed Shel Shrager and Guy McElwaine that "spirit and morale are high here, everybody believes we have a great picture and tries his best." I also recommended changing the start date of the huge 81-day schedule from December 12 to December 15 (the 12th was Kenyan Independence Day, a national holiday). We were locked and loaded. We just hoped that Coca-Cola/Columbia was.

Getting the Green Light

WE RETURNED TO LOS ANGELES confident that all obstacles would be cleared in Kenya so we could make *Sheena* there. We needed that before we could get the green light (approval) from Columbia. In fact, we needed two green lights: one from Columbia itself and another from their owner, the Coca-Cola Company.

The first thing I did when I got back was head to my office to figure the budget. It's a complex process that takes experience and time. I showed up at the studio to work on it. It happened to be on Yom Kippur, the holiest holiday in all of Judaism when, as you know, Jews are not allowed to work. The studio lot was absolutely empty. At the gate, I was happy to see that God was not on duty and I just had to say hello to the guard who I knew very well. I felt guilty working on Yom Kippur. Then I thought about how many people would get jobs because of the film and how many families would have an income because of what we were doing. When I realized this, and how important the film would be for Kenya, even though it was rationalization, I felt less guilty doing the budgets, the scheduling board, and other details that you give the studio in order for them to approve production.

Budgeting a film is never formulaic. Despite more than a century of effort by Hollywood studio bean counters to impose order on production, every film is different. Even a sequel is different than the original movie. To budget *Sheena* we needed to plan for all the elements that go into a production: large items like construction materials, crew and actor salaries, travel, and accommodations; medium-sized things like costumes, props, and make up supplies; and seemingly smaller things like letterheads, director's chairs, and even the 16mm film that would be a prop in a laboratory sequence. We also knew that this movie was so large and complex that it had to be shot with three units at the same time: a main unit with the actors, a second unit with the animals, and a third unit capturing stunts.

Few people stop to think that everything you see in a movie that isn't the natural scenery has to be brought there on purpose and paid for (although nowadays the scenery can be computer-generated). You literally must see the film in your head while reading the script in order to get an accurate budget breakdown. Today there are computer programs that help, but you still need experience to know what you're doing. I had already persuaded the studio that I had that experience; now I had to persuade myself.

I met with Frank Price. He was an interesting man. Before taking over the reins of Columbia Pictures, he had been a success in television, writing on such series as *The Tall Man* and *The Virginian,* and then executive producer of

Ironside, *Rich Man, Poor Man*, and several TV movies. Now he was running a major Hollywood studio.

The first thing he asked me was, "How was your recce to Kenya? How was it with John?" Then he saw that I was carrying a sheath of papers and we talked about the budget. I briefed him about our locations and about the assistance that we would get from the government and military of Kenya. I also told him that we would have to bring our animals from Hollywood to the African jungle. Like other people who ask me about that to this day, I explained to him why we needed to bring our animals that we can train rather than take a chance with the wild animal citizens of the jungle.

"So what is your conclusion about shooting in Kenya?" he finally asked. "Can we make do with a budget of $14 million?" I looked at him and thought to myself, "If I tell him yes we can, I advance my career and the movie's gonna be made. If I say no, then he would say, 'Thank you very much for your opinion' and I would be, along with hundreds of other people, unemployed." So I said, "Yes we can, knowing in my heart that making a movie with John Guillermin would be very hard to come in on budget, which was the main reason of getting this job.

As soon as I told him we could do it, he said, "I'm glad you think you can make this movie." I had the feeling that it was now going to become a "go" picture and I was very happy. But before he let me go he asked me, "How did you do with Guillermin?"

I said, "Oh, we had a great time together and we feel confident that we can make the movie." It was the truth, but it had stretch marks.

People often ask why a film goes over budget. As I noted above, even though Hollywood has been making movies for over a century, there are many variables that can affect the final cost. What if it rains? What if an actor or director gets sick or has to be replaced? What if locations are suddenly no longer available? What if one of more unions go on strike? And those are just the major obstacles. Other items that can wildly affect a budget are the price of construction materials, laboratory costs, special effects, accidents, and misbehaving actors or crew, any of which can also increase the cost of a film. None of these can be predicted and only a few can be anticipated. This is particularly true for filming in foreign territories like Africa.

John and I set up offices at the Burbank studio so we could hit the ground running once we got the official green light. It didn't take long after my meeting with Frank Price for Guy McElwaine to call. He first spoke to Guillermin and told him it was a "go" movie. Surprisingly, John took the news without emotion. He was very cool and suspicious, as he was whenever he got compliments. He handed the phone to me, saying, "Guy wants to speak with you." Guy's words are still in my ears: "Go make the movie." At that point, our step deals became pay-or-play. Needless to say, John and I were happy and shook hands at the decision. We would make *Sheena*. And the fact that it was Guy who called was especially promising in that, prior to coming to Columbia, Guy had been a highly successful agent with ICM—International Creative Management, one of Hollywood's top agencies. His relationship with the industry's creative personnel was valuable for Columbia Pictures and they offered him the job, taking him out of the agency business. Fortunately for us, as I noted before, one of Guy's major clients had been John Guillermin.

John's and my first move was to go to London where the studio's British casting associate, Maggie Cartier, would arrange auditions. (American casting was handled by the venerable Mike Fenton and Jane Feinberg.)

The London trip reminded me of something I had said to my wife, Ani. Seven years earlier I had finished working with the famous director Otto Preminger (*Exodus, Anatomy of a Murder*) on his film called *Rosebud* and he had invited us to London from Israel where he was doing the movie's post-production. Preminger stayed at the Dorchester, one of the world's great hotels. Not only that, he had his own suite (number 600). That night he invited Ani and me to have dinner with him and I saw how the hotel staff behaved toward him when he entered. It was "Hello, Mr. Preminger," "This way, Mr. Preminger," "Thank you, Mr. Preminger," and "I'm kissing your ass, Mr. Preminger," all of which made Preminger very, very happy. He liked when people noticed him. He was showing off in his suite, showing us bottles of wine with his name on them. He was bragging like a little child that made it big-time in Hollywood. We were about to go to dinner and he said, "I'm just going to get my coat and we'll go to dinner at the famous White Elephant Restaurant in London." As he went into the other room for his coat, I whispered in Ani's ear, "One day we will be here in this suite." Ani looked at me like I was crazy. And so, when the woman from Columbia's travel department called to give me a choice of where to stay during our

London trip, they said, "Do you want to go to the Hilton?" and named several other hotels. I said, "Could you find out about the Dorchester, suite number 600?"

She checked with the hotel and called me back. "It's available, Mr. Ben-Ami, but it's expensive."

I said, very nicely, "Please get it for me." And she did.

When Ani visited me in London while we were making *Sheena*, you should have seen her smile when we walked into the Preminger Suite. (I wish she had been more impressed with the room, but we had ridden up in the elevator with Rod Stewart. Why Rod Stewart? Because he was staying there, too. Oh well.)

First thing after checking into London, John and I headed to the office of Colgems Pictures International, the Columbia subsidiary in Europe under whose auspices we were making the picture. I met with their accountant to set up bank accounts, fill out paperwork, and get instructions from him on payroll, expenses, and the numerous other details of getting a production going. One of the advantages of working with a studio was that I never had to worry about getting around London. A man named Michael Marx was my chauffeur. I couldn't believe that seven years after leaving Israel's modest film industry I was a real, live Hollywood producer traveling in a limousine.

Maggie Cartier had done her casting job well. She brought in a series of talented international actors who were living in England. Trevor Thomas was a well-established British television actor with credits ranging from *Dr. Who* to several *BBC Playhouse* dramas. He was cast as Prince Otwani, the villain who has his brother killed in order to take over the country's resources. *Sheena* would be his first feature film. For King Jabalani, John selected Jamaica-born Clifton Jones, whose acting background included British dramas and thrillers. The icy mercenary Jorgensen was played by John Forgeham who had been both good guys and bad guys in many British productions including *The Italian Job*. And France Zobda, from Martinique, played the scheming Countess Zanda.

Our greatest challenge was finding the right person to play the important part of the Shaman who raises Sheena and instructs her in the ways of the jungle. The Shaman had to be regal, proud, beautiful, and exude a magical quality.

"I have someone for you to see," Maggie told John on the phone, "but I don't know if she can carry the role on her shoulders."

"Why not?" asked John.

"Because I don't know how much acting experience she has."

"Oh."

"But she is a lawyer, a diplomat, a model, and the former Secretary of State to Idi Amin, the Ugandan dictator. She had to flee the country and wound up here."

John's curiosity was piqued. "Bring her in," he said.

"And she's also a real princess," Maggie added.

"*Absolutely* bring her in!"

When Princess Elizabeth of Toro arrived for her audition (which was more of a meet-and-greet than an audition), we saw that Maggie had been right about her. Elizabeth was a very beautiful African woman whose exile from Uganda, caused by Idi Amin, had put her at economic disadvantage. And yet her bearing was not diminished by her situation.

Elizabeth wrote about her audition in her 1989 autobiography, *The Odyssey of an African Princess*, remembering that, "John Guillermin, the director…could not contain his excitement" and, although she was too young for the role of the Shaman in the later scenes, ageing makeup would get around it. The script was another matter. "It was badly written," she wrote, "but for me, *Sheena* expressed a certain truth, a certain reality, that an indigenous culture, a way of life of a people, had suffered an assault at the hands of an alien one. The role of the Shaman, the defender of the indigenous culture of *Sheena*, had parallels with my own life and what had come to pass for Africa and our people."[6]

Princess Elizabeth of Toro brought her past to her role. She was the daughter of Rukidi III of Toro, one of the kings of the four tribes that ruled Uganda before it became a country in 1962. She graduated from Cambridge University to become Uganda's first female lawyer, and was appointed foreign minister and then Ambassador to the United States in 1974 by her country's brutal dictator, Idi Amin (who proposed marriage to her, which she rejected). In February 1975, she was forced to flee Uganda when Amin charged her with moral turpitude, but she returned in 1979 only to flee again in 1980 with her husband Prince Wilberforce Nyabongo.[7]

This was our Shaman.

---

6. Elizabeth Nyabongo, *Elizabeth of Toro: The Odyssey of an African Princess*, NY: Touchstone, 1989.

7. Nyabongo played the airplane pilot who brings Vic and Fletch to Tigora in their first scene.

In America, the casting was also going apace. Donovan Scott, an effortlessly funny young man, became the hero's best friend, Fletcher, who captures Prince Otwani's assassination on film. Fresh from the hit movie *Police Academy*, Donovan raised the spirits of everyone on the production. He also had the gift of turning scripted joke lines that weren't funny into dialogue that actually got laughs. I thought that every movie set should have a guy like him.

"I was originally just called in for an audition," Scott—who we all called "Scotty"—recalled, "but when I went in to audition, I thought I was doing it by myself. I brought in a camera and a pith helmet because I thought I was supposed to be the photographer. I just couldn't wait to audition because Africa was a childhood dream of mine. I always wanted to go, I always wanted to be part of that adventure. I saw every Tarzan Johnny Weissmuller movie and I actually saw a Tarzan movie of John Guillermin's, *Tarzan's Greatest Adventure*, which I really liked. So I was excited to meet him and excited about the project. I didn't care what I had to play as long as I got to go to Africa."

"When I did the audition, it was a total bust because another actor came in and we read the roles together. I don't even think he wanted to do the film. He was not prepared and totally threw my performance off. I went back home, almost crying, and called my agents and said, 'You gotta get me in again. You gotta get me in again.' They said, 'We can't do that' and I said, 'No, no, no, get me back in again. I want to get this.' So they called up and they got me back in again. I actually asked John, when we got to Africa, 'How did I get the role?' And he said, 'Your enthusiasm is really what pushed me forward on you.'"

Other parts, plus the scores of extras and dancers, would be local hires in Kenya. There were numerous parts to fill, and we would begin looking for candidates when we returned to Africa.

Our second recce was more elaborate than the first. Now that we had a green light from the studio, we needed to start preproduction. After several days in London, John and I arranged to rendezvous in Nairobi. We again stayed at the Norfolk in suites next to the luxurious balcony. Guillermin and I took a rest, lounging on armchairs on an incredibly colorful porch, the kind enjoyed by generations of British Crown Princes or their khaki costume designers, colonists of all races and times. On such a balcony, deliberately cut off from the filth of the Kenyan street, you are not just sitting but drifting in the flavors of exotic liquor, the ocean of whiskey and cognac, or, in my case, just dropping another can of Coca-Cola. It was not just cold and sweet; the waiter at the Norfolk served it in a crystal glass with an orange slice, giving it an essence far above that of its customary red can.

Soon we were joined by the team he had chosen to work with him from among the world's finest artisans:

- Pasqualino de Santis, Director of Photography, Oscar-winner for *Romeo and Juliet* (1969);

- Rémy Julienne, French Stunt Coordinator specializing in car chases and crashes;

- Miguel Gil, Assistant Director who had made other films with John;

- Paul Aratow, the producer who had been developing *Sheena* for eight years;

- Christian Ferry, Associate Producer and Production Manager, long associated with John;

- Peter Murton, Production Designer (*The Ruling Class, The Man with the Golden Gun, Dracula, Superman II*);

- Lorenzo Semple, Jr., screenwriter who did the final version of the script.

Each person's job on a recce is both specific and general: first determine his or her department's requirements for the film, and then to make sure that everyone works together toward the same end.

As for me, I had to make sure everyone had what he or she needed. By the time the film rolled in Africa, I had Caterpillar tractors building roads, runways, and fields; construction crews building bridges, roads, and sets; three planes and helicopters; and contractors setting up storage facilities, offices, communications, wardrobe, and shops. We were coming into a country that didn't have a filmmaking industry (I would later work to improve that) and had very few people with filmmaking experience, yet by the time we left a great many people would have skills.

We also knew that there was no way we were going to bring this movie in for $14 million. At that moment we realized that it was us versus Coca-Cola/Columbia.

Coca-Cola wanted value for their blocked funds. The picture had dragged on for so many years under different managements and run up so many development costs that Coca-Cola/Columbia had to make it or else write off an embarrassing dollar figure as a business loss.

An incident on this second recce told me that Guillermin was not only fully in control but completely dedicated to making the picture—at any cost. We came to a clearing and John stated, "We will shoot the scene here." That's how he talked, nothing was negotiable. As he described the scene, Paul Aratow, the producer who had been pushing the project since the mid-1970s, jumped in and said, "Well, John, in the comic strip and in the other scripts, this is not how it should be done." John let him finish and then told him, "If you keep doing this to me, you will work another eight years on this movie. So what I suggest is that you have a nice office on the Columbia lot. You go back tomorrow to America, to your office, and you sit in your office, and I'll see you at the premiere." I have to give Aratow credit; that's just what he did. He made the big mistake of intruding on the director's territory, a director that had a different concept of how to shoot the scene. He didn't know what I have learned through the years, that if you give a script to ten directors they will give you back ten different movies. Paul was a nice guy, knowledgeable, intellectual, and it was a pleasure to talk to him. But he realized that he was never going to be friends with Guillermin, and that, if he wanted to get the movie made after all he had been through with it, the best thing was to shut up and head home.

Did John overreact? Perhaps. Many directors make a point of firing somebody early-on to establish their authority and to breed fear in a crew. Getting rid of a producer (especially one whom we all knew had no power) was just a ploy. But Guillermin was like that. He was a contrarian. He was a man who, if you said it's night, he would challenge you and prove it's day. Life was boring for him if nothing happened, and if it didn't happen on its own, he would make it happen himself.

He made people prove their mettle. Not everybody could. There was a notable instance where all the department heads accompanied John on an aerial recce. I had to stay behind, but I heard about it afterward. In mid-air, John insisted that the pilot let him take the controls. John was an accredited pilot and had flown with the RAF, but that was small comfort to his passengers when he started maneuvering the large aircraft as if it was a fighter plane. He decided, when he saw a herd of gazelles, to dive-bomb them and chase them across the savannah. When he landed the aircraft, Miguel Gil—the assistant director who had worked with Guillermin on previous films—came to my office. He was shaking and his face was white. He said, "Yoram, I quit. I am going to my room and taking my stuff. Guillermin is crazy. He almost killed all of us." He headed home the same day.

After Miguel left, we hired Patrick Clayton who was a good Assistant Director and had a wicked sense of humor. Being English, he understood John to a tee. At one point the set was so noisy—so many different nationalities talking in their own tongues, including Maa, the language spoken by Kenya's Maasai tribe—that John finally said, "Patrick, tell them to shut the fuck up. I can't hear myself think."

"Right," said Patrick. "The next person who opens his mouth is gonna go back to England."

Naturally, somebody spoke. "Fire that man," John said, keeping his word.

"Already done, sir," said Patrick.

"Good," said John. "Who was it?"

Patrick smiled. "One big Maasai on his way to England."

Terrific Tanya

THAT FIRST IMAGE OF TANYA ROBERTS in her leather bikini, the one she wore as she walked through the valley of the soundstages at Columbia studios, did not leave my mind for even a moment during production of *Sheena*. That is because the leather bikini never left Tanya Roberts (except for two brief scenes) in the entire movie. Although she was the star of the film, and movie stars supposedly have it cushy, what she had to go through as "Queen of the Jungle" was something no star should have to endure. But she did, and everyone who worked on the picture marveled at her dedication.

Barely twenty-eight when she came to Kenya, she was called upon to swing from vines, fire flaming arrows, scurry up trees, climb cliffs, handle snakes, walk with lions, act with elephants, hold the screen opposite a chimpanzee, and ride a horse bareback—all in a costume that constantly exposed her to the sun, wind, and dust. (Riding bareback is a particular ordeal; the rough horsehair is immensely irritating on bare thighs. For this reason, for long shots a stunt rider was used.) Tanya did everything she was called to do, including act. A real Wonder Woman.

By the time she swung into *Sheena*, she had already played "Julie Rogers" on Columbia's hit TV series *Charlie's Angels* and this gave her both visibility and credibility when the role of Sheena was being cast. Tanya exuded classic star appeal: a beautiful face, a beautiful figure, a beautiful girl.

"She was game," praises animal trainer Jules Sylvester, who worked with her and the menagerie, getting them used to each other. "She tried very hard." Her husband Barry Roberts was with her on location, and the bond between the two of them got her through the often-grueling shoot.

She was never less than professional. Her husband Barry and I became friends, which was important in a place like the jungles of Africa. He wasn't friends with everybody, however. One day I had to intervene in a fist fight between him and John Guillermin that suddenly erupted near the camera. I stepped between them and kept them apart. I never learned what triggered it. Barry was a good provider and a good husband and was on the set at all times making sure nothing happened to Tanya, but something must have transpired between takes because he and John were going at it. It was a very hot day and I remember that the camera had a high umbrella to shade it. I pulled them apart and let them cool down. To this day I don't know the reason for the outburst.

Tanya was well worth protecting. Born Victoria Leigh Blum in the Bronx, New York, in 1955, she left high school at age 15 with her heart set on adventure. She and her mother lived briefly in Toronto, and Tanya admitted to enjoying her "wild and crazy" teen years, traveling around the country and getting married far too young in 1971. (Her mother-in-law had the marriage annulled.)[8] Becoming more settled, she returned to New York took acting classes with influential teachers Lee Strasberg and Uta Hagen and landed small roles in off-Broadway revivals.

Given her captivating blue eyes and heart-stopping beauty, she was a natural for modeling, and landed a number of accounts including Cool-Ray® Sunglasses, Clairol hair products, and Ultra-Brite® toothpaste. She also earned money as a dance instructor at the Arthur Murray Dance Studio where she developed a flair for Latin dancing.

In 1974 she married psychology student Barry Roberts. It was literally the movies that brought them together; they were waiting in a line for movie tickets and started talking. (The title of the film has been lost to time and romance.) Soon she proposed to him and the couple headed for Los Angeles where Tanya made the rounds and her husband sought work as an actor and writer.

"I told Barry, 'Listen, baby, I'm going to be a star if it kills me, and I'm taking you with me.'" she told entertainment writer Jacob Shelton. "He didn't laugh—lucky for him I tried out for a part in every major movie for three years."[9] While her husband switched from psychology to screenwriting, Tanya (by now professionally called Tanya Roberts) gained increasing visibility between 1976 and 1979 in roles in such films as *Zuma Beach*, *The Yum-Yum Girls*, *The Private Files of J. Edgar Hoover*, and the cult comedy *Tourist Trap*. In 1980 she became one of *Charlie's Angels* during that landmark show's fifth season. "It was my first steady

---

8. IMDb biography by Ray Angelo, Ray Angelo, rangelo@oeb.harvard.edu
9. Jacob Shelton, https://groovyhistory.com/tanya-roberts-bond-girl-sheena-beastmaster-then-and-now, January 11, 2020

job, and it launched my career," she told the *Charlie's Angels* tribute website. She auditioned twice and "I did a dramatic scene where I had to cry, which was no problem because when I was younger I could cry at the drop of a hat."

She made sixteen episodes for *Charlie's Angels* before the series was canceled, then starred opposite Marc Singer in 1982's *The Beastmaster*. That role—plus a *Playboy* publicity tie-in spread—brought her to the attention of Columbia's Frank Price and Guy McElwaine who felt she would make a perfect Sheena. All she had to do was dye her naturally brown hair blonde (to match the character's description in the script) and look good in a leather bikini. No problemo.

Tanya's post-*Sheena* career includes a run on *That '70s Show* as "Midge Pinciotti," a housewife of the era gaining confidence in herself with the arrival of the Women's Movement. She made TV appearances on *High Tide*, *Burke's Law*, *Pajama Party*, and *Silk Stalkings*. She also returned to the theatre in off-Broadway productions of *A View From a Bridge*, *The Hydes of March*, and *Sextette*.

Working in Kenya opened Tanya to a world she had never seen before. "I'm an animal freak, so filming *Sheena* was the most fun for me," she told Shelton. "I got to work with all of the animals and spend time in exotic places that were free from hunters."[10] It also opened her eyes to the plight of children in East Africa.

"People in Uganda and other developing countries are sacrificing for us every day," she wrote on her blog. "I can't believe that Uganda, Congo, Sudan, and Rwanda have had twenty million deaths in the last twenty years and still

---

10. Ibid

counting. But it's the homeless children who are suffering the most." She promised to return to Africa to bring light to the human suffering.[11]

She also visited Bosnia and Kosovo in the USO's Celebrity "Handshake" tour, thanking the troops (and no doubt making them yearn for home), and plays in celebrity golf tournaments.

I kept in touch with Tanya and her husband Barry after filming stopped. While in England, she spent some of her *Sheena* salary on a beautiful Rolls-Royce with right-hand British steering that she later had shipped to America. Back in the States, my wife Ani and I had several dinners with the Robertses at their home in Westwood. On one memorable evening we found ourselves sitting with Dr. Timothy Leary, the well-known LSD popularizer. (No, we didn't trip.)

Tanya wasn't able to attend the premiere of *Sheena* in 1984; she was in Europe shooting the James Bond movie, *A View to a Kill*. I like to think that I had a hand in getting her that job. While I was in post-production at Pinewood Studios in England, my office was next to the office of Albert "Cubby" Broccoli, the producer of the James Bond films, who was prepping his next 007 production. "How is Tanya?" he asked me casually, one producer to another. I didn't hesitate for one moment. "Oh,. She's fantastic," I answered, and *A View to a Kill* became her next picture. She was a Bond girl opposite Roger Moore, and you can't do better than that.

But for me, of course, she will always be Sheena. In a leather bikini.

---

11. http://www.tanyaroberts.biz/en.blog.html, September 14, 2016.

Ted Wass

TED WASS HIT THE JUNGLE RUNNING. Signed for the role of Vic Casey only days before we started shooting, he, his wife, actress Janet Margolin (*David and Lisa*) and their baby, Julian, arrived in Nairobi and immediately began working. It wasn't easy for him. Unlike the breakthrough situation comedy *Soap*, on which Ted had appeared in over seventy episodes between 1977 and 1981, *Sheena* wouldn't shoot in a comfortable ABC-TV studio. Yet he acclimated with remarkable smoothness and speed.

Ted had won wide acclaim on *Soap* playing gangster-wannabe Danny Dallas. It was his first major television job, having come fresh from Broadway starring as Danny Zuko in *Grease*. On *Soap* the then-twenty-five year old Wass more than held his own against scene-stealers Katharine Helmond, Billy Crystal, Roscoe Lee Browne, Jay Johnson, Dinah Manoff, and Richard Mulligan.

Sheena was a change of pace for Ted. It was a romantic lead with comic and action elements, and he more than pleased us. Guillermin and Columbia agreed that Ted was right for the role. As a man, he was a professional, really a professional, a nice guy, and nice to everybody. There was no "star" attitude. He, Tanya, and Donovan Scott got along well with each other and the crew, working as a team despite the often unpleasant weather and landscape conditions. But we also took good care of them; they stayed at the Norfolk Hotel, they had their Winnebagos, and their assistants took care of their needs. Ted and his family, in particular, could venture freely in public, go shopping, and take safari tours without being recognized by the public (*Soap* hadn't yet made it to Kenya).

I am pleased to say that Ted has said that he has a warm spot for me and for the work I did producing *Sheena*, providing support and helping him get through it all. I feel just as warmly toward him; between the animals, the locations, and the other challenges, we had a good relationship and developed mutual respect.

Following *Sheena*, Ted appeared in several films and television shows, including as Mayim Bialyk's father on the TV series *Blossom*. It was during that show's four-year run that he began directing as well as acting and, since that show wrapped, has directed scores of TV movies and episodes.

Ted and his wife, Janet, had a second child, Matilda. Sadly, Janet died in 1993. In 1996 he married producer Nina Wass (nee Fineberg). The couple has a daughter, Stella.

Flying Wild Animals To Africa

OVER THE YEARS, when I have told people that we had to bring our own animals to Africa to make *Sheena*, I would get the strangest looks. Didn't Africa already have animals? they would ask. Oddly enough, the answer was both Yes and No. This is one of the most fascinating and least understood aspects of making *Sheena*.

Yes, Africa is full of animals, but they are *wild* animals. There is no way to let them interact safely with actors. Therefore we engaged Hubert Wells whose company, Animal Actors of Hollywood, has provided creatures to practically every important film since he immigrated here from Hungary. Hubert has called his experience on *Sheena* the pinnacle of his professional career. I recognized his expertise and did not deny him and his crew anything that they needed. In his memoir, *Lights, Camera, Lions* (NY: Morgan James Publishing, 2017), Hubert wrote that this was the hardest film that he ever worked on, but added, "One more pleasant surprise, on *Sheena* I did not have to fight for every penny. 'If you need it, you shall have it' was the surprising answer from the producer, Yoram Ben-Ami." Hubert then added, "To hell with the critics, *Sheena* is my favorite movie."

This was years before computer-generated animals would become a movie mainstay. In those days, our animals had to be flesh-and-blood, not ones and zeros. Bringing animals to Africa is complicated. They need to be safely transported, quarantined, fed, and protected. Nobody wants to have an animal get sick or die at any point during production. For this important task we hired a team of highly trained animal handlers to work with Hubert.

In the film, Sheena rides a zebra (Marika), has a personal elephant (Chango, played by Sita), and a chimpanzee sidekick (Tita, played by Caranga). She mentally summons animals by putting her hand to her forehead, concentrating, and sending "radio waves" that the animals understand. She learned this from the Shaman. In this way, she gets help from a rhinoceros and calls on a flock of flamingos to rescue her. All of this required extensive prep. We learned, for example, that you cannot train giraffes, rhinos, or zebras. How, then, was Sheena to ride a zebra in the film? The logistics were so complex that we had to assign a separate unit (camera, crew, trainers, support systems) to film all the animal sequences. This was supervised by the experienced naturalist and filmmaker Jack Couffer. John Guillermin, of course, was responsible for everything overall, but he spent the bulk of his time filming the scenes with the actors. We also had a third unit that filmed the stunts. It was run by seasoned stuntman/second unit director Max Kleven.

Well before cameras rolled, we had our paws full. The animal cast that we had to ship to Kenya included a rhinoceros, an elephant, three leopards, four lions, four chimpanzees, twelve flamingos, and three beautiful Arabian horses. Because these exotic animals could not possibly travel with the poodles on regular commercial airliners, we had to arrange for them on a combination of cargo planes and charter flights. You cannot imagine what was involved in taking relatively tame animals from their comfortable home in Los Angeles and expect them to get along with their wild cousins in Africa. On top of that, we had to train them to act in a setting that was unfamiliar to them. Well before the start of filming, we sent our star animals to Africa. The Lufthansa jumbo jet in America was loaded: an elephant who could learn one trick every week like tipping a tree over, dropping a house, or flipping a bad guy in the air with his trunk.

It was especially important for us to bring "our" animals because, on March 14, 1983, Kenyan President Daniel arap Moi—perhaps heading off a controversy—issued a statement that he "would not allow wild animals to be trapped, exported, or put in orphanages. "I have been informed," he said, "that the Wildlife department had issued trapping permits and I am still awaiting to be told the reasons for doing it." It was a pro-forma statement in that, other than the animals we were bringing from the States, we had already contracted with African-based animals currently living in preserves under human care. They were not "orphans."

On November 24, 1983 we met with D.M. (Daniel) Sindiyo, Director of the Wildlife Conservation and Management Department of Kenya. At that time, we proposed bringing "tamed and trained" animals into the park for filming. We assured him that the animals would be kept in a compound built on a selected site between Rhino Bridge and Elephant Bridge with fence, cages, and a camp for trainers. We also promised to grade roads before and after filming, asked to be able to enter and leave the park before and after public hours, and wanted permission to fire blank rounds and other detonations in the Aberdare Park. Watchful of his responsibilities but mindful of the benefits to Kenya, Mr. Sindiyo agreed. Later fees of $120,000 and $117,400 Ks. (Kenyan shillings) were paid for licenses and park entry fees, respectively.

In preparation for the arrival of our menagerie, the team built a fortified enclosure in the Kenya National Park with eucalyptus poles buried five feet in the ground, cemented, and wired together. It wasn't long before our presence became known. On the first night, wild lions arrived and tried to attack our animals in the compound. We had invaded their territory. From then on, every night, we had to light flares and shoot light bombs to scare them away.

A lion's growl may be impressive at the beginning of an MGM movie, but there is nothing more terrifying than the real thing coming out of the darkness of the jungle. Imagine being a zebra and hearing that sound arising from the bush and knowing it's meant for you! We insured the animals for millions of dollars, just as we did our film's human stars and crew. We also had to make sure that all of them were fed, received medical attention, and could be safely housed as we moved their compounds from one location to another, miles apart. We had a special construction crew of fifteen people doing this at all times.

Every animal has its own craziness and demands, and each animal has to adapt to its new environment. Likewise, the cast and crew had to work together with the animals, no matter where: jungle, mountains, wetlands, and plains.

Many real-life stories add to the on-screen story of *Sheena*. One that we had to address the moment we set up shop, weeks before it would be seen on screen, was scene 96A. Ted Wass played the co-starring role of Vic Casey. On paper, scene 96A looked like a cinch:

Shots of wonderful elephants. We find Vic and Sheena walking amidst them. Vic immensely awed, his eyes wary on the enormous beasts so close alongside.

John and Pasqualino chose to cover it in a master, two-shot, over-the-shoulder reverses, and close-ups with a few cut-aways of the herd. Sounds easy, but it wasn't.

The first thing we all needed was a herd of at least a hundred wild elephants to come out of the jungle. In order to get them to stay in the background, we first had to attract them there. It wasn't something for which you could send out a casting call. In consultation with an English biology professor, we realized that Napoleon's statement that "an army travels on its stomach" also applies to wild elephants, and so does Pavlov's theory of conditioning. A month before filming the scene, we daily brought a huge truck full of tomatoes and carrots and spread them across the ground where we wanted the wild elephants to be in the background. We had to calculate where the sun was going to be and the angle at which we had to shoot Tanya and Ted on the scheduled day. We left food every day at 4 o'clock. The wild elephants learned that 4 o'clock was feeding time. A month later, when we shot the scene at 4 o'clock in the afternoon, the elephants were so busy chowing down that they didn't notice our trucks, our technicians, and our actors. They stayed in the background. Of course, starting the day after we finished the scene, it was a cruel, "I'm all right, Jack" and they were back foraging on their own.

All of this effort was so Sheena could tell Vic, "It's the dry season. They cannot find enough to eat" and for Vic to respond, "That big guy in front…he's looking at me."

At the same time we did that scene, we grabbed a shot (Scenes 24 and 25) with young Sheena for the early "growing up" montage.

The elephant accompanying Sheena and Vic in that scene was our own Sita. Sita, which means "six" in Swahili, arrived tamed and trained and ready to work. We brought her and her trainer from a circus in America. In the film she played Chango, Sheena's personal helper in tough situations. She had to be trained one trick at a time, and it took a few days to teach her each one. Sita's first big scene was crashing into the jail where the Shaman, Sheena's mentor, had been placed by the police who planned to blame her for the assassination of King Jabalani of Tigora. It was a night shoot in the Karura Forest, and the script said:

EXT. AZAN JAIL - NIGHT

Not any Alcatraz, just a ramshackle structure at the edge of the bush. Wire perimeter fence around it. A SUDDEN SOUND shatters the night: THE MIGHTY TRUMPETING OF AN ELEPHANT. Only sensational. Here comes this elephant out of the jungle like a fucken tank, knocking trees down, charging toward the jailhouse. Galloping hooves. Sheena on Marika (her zebra) emerging from the floodlit dust in her leather bikini, golden hair streaming as she comes up alongside Chango the Elephant.

Sita performed like a trooper, smashing the wall to smithereens so Sheena could rush in to comfort the Shaman, who was on the ground after being beaten by police. Sheena scoops her up and together they rode off on Marika while Sita finishes the job by collapsing a water tower on the jail, pushing her way through a wire fence, and following Sheena into the jungle, stopping along the way to bend the rotor blade on one of Otwani's helicopters so it can't chase them.

Sita had another big scene which was set in South Hell's Gate, Naivasha (Scene 100-103) in which she topples a tree across a mountain road, blocking Jorgensen's convoy. She gets her orders telepathically from Sheena:

Elephant very still, ears flapping slowly, listening to no sound we can perceive. He starts running suddenly... Narrow here, steep bolder-strewn banks. SOUND OF VEHICLES coming this way. Chango the Elephant is butting mightily against a tree. It's a monster tree, it starts toppling...

An old Hollywood adage goes, "a tree is a tree," but apparently John Guillermin never heard it because he wanted a special tree for the stunt. He needed a tree that would block the road so the bad guys in their trucks could not move it to follow Sheena and Vic. A *papier-mâché* tree wouldn't work, so we dispatched special scouts to look for a real tree that was at least fifty feet tall and heavy enough to do the job. When they found one 100 miles away from South Hell's Gate where the scene was to be shot, it took two huge flatbed trucks combined to haul it there and a construction crane to lift it into position.

Another animal adventure that started before we began shooting involved a chimpanzee. When we arrived in Kenya in 1983, the country was still settling down from the August 1982 coup attempt. The coup failed when soldiers who were supposed to topple President Daniel arap Moi failed to do so and the entire plan collapsed. Retribution was swift and vigilance was still high when our filmmaking company arrived at Nairobi Airport.

Of all the celebrities who stepped off the plane, none attracted more attention than Caranga, our big chimp. Ever the attention hog, Caranga performed for the fans, waving, screaming, and jumping in and out of the car that we were using. Everyone noticed how he responded to Hubert's spoken commands. Clearly, he understood human speech.

Now flash forward to a story that made Hubert, Jules Sylvester (one of Hubert's assistants), and me laugh. Hubert, Jules, and Caranga were driving to a location at Samburu Game Preserve. They stopped at the main gate and the guard came out from his guard shack to greet them, handing them a book for them to sign for entry. Hubert and Jules signed and handed it back, but this did not satisfy the gate guard. The guard pointed to Caranga and says, "He must sign, too."

"But he's a chimp," Hubert said.

"That does not matter," said the guard. "He must sign."

Even though it was weird, Hubert didn't want to argue with the guard, so he handed the book and a pen to Caranga, who made a mark that the guard determined was a signature. And they all drove into the park.

That isn't the end of the story. The caravan made it to the main office of Samburu Game Preserve and Hubert told the head of the preserve what had happened at the gate, expecting him to laugh. He didn't. The guard had already phoned up from the gate and the head of the preserve had become deadly serious. "I want to talk to Mr. Wells," he said. Taking Hubert aside, he informed him, in his most official tone of voice, "at no time can this chimpanzee be loose and walking around the hills."

"Nothing will be running around loose out here," Hubert assured him.

Then the man said, "Because, you see, we have baboons here and at no time must this chimpanzee talk to these baboons because you know how baboons lie."

At first Hubert thought the man was joking. It finally dawned on them that when they had arrived at the airport and the newspapers reported that Caranga could understand English, the Kenyan official worried that he might also be able to translate from baboon to chimp, and thereafter to English, and so might pass inside information that the baboons had witnessed about what was happening in Kenya. It kind of made sense. Baboons like to watch. They sit there in a group and stare at you. What this had to do with getting a chimpanzee to sign a guest book still escapes me. It makes me wonder what the baboons might have actually seen that the game preserve official didn't want us to know.

One of our most headstrong actors was Big H (named after Hubert), a five thousand pound rhinoceros with a huge horn that Hubert housed in his California compound. He was shipped along with the rest of the animals by way of New Jersey and London before arriving in Kenya. He got to us a day late, however, because, when he hit London, Queen Elizabeth needed the plane and Big H had to be bumped to another flight.

Describing Big H as a movie lover would be wrong. He hated the job and kept trying to escape. Finally, one day, he put his horn under the fence posts of the compound where he was quartered and lifted the twelve-inch logs right out of the ground, and tore out into the jungle.

The animal unit had to shut down for two days while Big H was "persuaded" to return. At the start, Ted Wass, Donovan Scott, and one of the makeup women volunteered for the posse.

"The three of them jumped in the back of the last of the three trucks to take off after the rhino," Scotty reports, "and we spent the rest of the day chasing down the rhino, darting the rhino so that he would not die because he was so hot and he was running away from us up hill. They only stay on trails so this one stayed in the road most of the time.

He finally got darted so that they could slow him down. I have the whole thing on video. It was the adventure of a lifetime; it was *Hatari* for me."

After chasing him for five miles, and clinging onto one of the vehicles, one of the handlers managed to fire a final tranquilizer dart into Big H with just enough juice in it to make him woozy but not go to sleep (how would you carry a 5,000-pound rhino back to camp?). One of the trainers managed to shine a flashlight into his eyes to blind him so that Sled Reynolds, another trainer, could lasso him and lead him back to the animal compound. At one point, still awake, Big H turned on one of the Land Cruisers, lowered his head, and jammed his horn under the front fender, and got stuck. Unable to pull it out, he tried lifting the vehicle with his 2,000-pound head.

After the movie wrapped, Hubert decided to donate "Big H" to the Kenya Game Department where he could live safely and make little rhinos. Sadly, five years later, he and his new herd were slaughtered for their horns by Somali poachers.

Living With Lions

EVEN THOUGH OUR FOUR LIONS were penned for their safety, they nevertheless fought at night with the wild lions who were attracted by their scent. Hubert posted guards to make sure neither side mingled with the other, and it's a good thing none of them did or weapons would have to have been fired. Our lions were trained, but not the way that Siegfried and Roy's lions were trained. Ours didn't jump through fiery hoops or sit politely on platforms, but they would go from one place to another on cue, roar on command, or sit still and look majestic. They would respond to hand signals, voice commands, or whip, and the reason they did it was for food. It goes like this:

fessionals, but because they shared a European sensibility (Hubert is Hungarian). Both men could let profanity fly one minute and brush it off the next. Hubert was good with wild animals, which probably explains why he got along so well with John and me.

In our original script there was a scene where little Sheena, age eight, for one of her daily chores, sticks her head inside a lion's mouth to brush its teeth. It wasn't a question of getting insurance, we simply did not want to place the girl in jeopardy, even with our trained lion. We even considered having a prosthetic lion's head made but it would have cost $100,000 for a few seconds of screen time, so it was better to cut the scene.

When it comes to feeding lions, like all cats, they eat meat. We were sometimes able to acquire great amounts of fresh meat from local veterinarians or safari parks who, instead of putting down enfeebled horses or cattle with lethal injections, would dispatch them with less toxic means and let them be slaughtered for lion feed.

Our closest and most tense encounter with lions during filming happened while shooting scene 76 in which reporter Vic Casey (Ted Wass) and his cameraman Fletch (Donovan Scott) follow Sheena into the Argenia Forest in the Aberdare National Park and have their Land Rover surrounded by lions. The script called for a "Big Old Lion" to come charging after Vic and Fletch and stop right in front of their vehicle.

FLETCH
N-n-nice lion...n-n-nice lion.

> VIC
> Make that plural.

And three more lions stalk out, growling, on all sides. Suddenly Sheena swings down on a vine, lands on the hood of the vehicle, looks the men in their frightened eyes, and utters the immortal words that every film critic made fun of—

> SHEENA
> Do you want to die?

—except it came out of Tanya's beautiful Bronx mouth sounding like:

> SHEENA
> Yo wanna doy?

Putting the lions aside for a moment, the matter of Sheena's/Tanya's accent, which was incompatible with her physical presence, would become the subject of critical comment when the picture opened, but it didn't loom as that important at the time. She was so game, so cooperative, and so giving in every aspect of making the picture that we accepted it as part of her considerable charm.

Donovan Scott was game, too. In fact, he was almost a meal for one of the lions who, as the scene progresses, sticks his huge, maned head into his driver's window and goes nose-to-nose with him. This was neither a stuffed model nor a special effect, but a real lion. Trained, sure, but real. I have to hand it to Donovan for bravery. Where he was pretending to be scared, he probably really was. What does a lion's breath smell like?

"It's a very meaty smell," Scotty now says, "and I was glad it wasn't *my* meat. The whole trick to that was that they had a cup of meat, raw meat, to my right between Ted and me, and I would reach down and palm the meat in my hand and then turn to the lion, and he would come in, bring his head in more, into a two-shot. One time I reached down and there was no more meat. When I'm feeding my dog or giving him treats or anything, when I'm done, I go, 'No more, no more,' and I shake my hand. So I put my hand down and I know the lion's watching me through the window, and I brought my hand up and shook it and went, 'Oh no, oh no,' and the whole 450-pound lion jumps into the car. He's smashing me. They yell, 'Cut! Cut! Cut!' and Guillermin says, 'Are you okay? Are you okay?' and I say [spoken through a squeezed mouth], 'Yes, I'm fine, I'm fine, please get the lion off my face.'"

And then it got more real than we wanted. Midway through shooting the scene, camera rolling, Hubert Wells carefully reached for his sidearm and called out, "Freeze! Nobody move!" The camera stopped turning and all 200 cast and crew eyes on the set shifted to two approaching lions *that were not ours*. They were wild. They had emerged from a steep hill and walked casually among the crowd of us as we stood frozen. Very, very scary. They approached our lead lioness and started sniffing her. We didn't know that our lioness was in heat, but they did. No one moved. Not even Guillermin. Hubert's deputy trainers pulled out their guns as a precaution. Our lioness was scared, too, and froze in her tracks while the visitors surveyed the scene.

They smelled her for three minutes. Our lion showed no interest in them (she was probably spoiled by dating Hollywood lions). Finally the visitors got bored, huffed with disinterest, and went away to continue being wild lions while we went back to making our movie.

You'd think that having a lion breathe in your face would put you off, but not Donovan Scott. He grew to love them. But he was still wary. He remembers that, later in the scene where he and Vic first encounter Sheena, the two men are supposed to lie on the ground while Sheena's lions and rhino keep them safe. Watching as the crew sets up the shot, Scotty noticed that the animal handlers were having trouble getting the rhino ready.

"They finally get it ready," he says, "and Ted and I are brought onto the set. There are three lions on the set: two on the car, one laying down next to me. I'm on the ground. Ted's on the ground. And then, all of a sudden, we see them digging a ditch underneath the Jeep. [I'm thinking] 'Hmm, that's interesting; I wonder what's going on under the Jeep.' Then they went over and they jammed the front door to the Jeep so it wouldn't close. And then they came over and said, 'Scotty, if the rhino doesn't stop where he's supposed to, you might need to roll underneath the Jeep and, Ted, you might need to jump into the Jeep; that's why the door is affixed so that it won't close.' We went, 'Oh, really?' They're laughing and talking and having a great time as they're bringing in the animal, the lions, and all that stuff, and they're setting up the cameras, and we're laughing and just before they get ready to go, we say, 'How do you train a rhino to stop on its mark?' And then we started to get a little nervous. Then we hear, 'Okay, stand by, the rhino's out, the rhino's coming down, get ready, here we go, roll cameras.' The rhino never paused for a second. It just kept running. I rolled under the car, Ted jumped into the Jeep, and the rhino was attacked by three lions—and went crazy! We were in a closed wooden fence to do the shoot and the rhino went over and took his little horn and took the bottom rung of the fence and flicked it like you would flick a cigarette and destroyed the entire fence and ran away. And I thought, 'Wow, if he could do that, what were we thinking?'"

Wild lions also made a nuisance of themselves at our camp compound when we were shooting on location. Often they would come at night, drawn by the scent of food (both in storage and on the hoof) and we had to chase them away with flares and the fog from CO_2 fire extinguishers.

"The lion and rhino compound was a five-minute drive from my tent," noted Hubert Wells. "[Jules Sylvester] and his African assistant, Boniface, stayed with the animals. The second night, about 2 a.m., I woke to the infernal noise of lions roaring, people shouting, and CO_2 fire extinguishers whooshing. I jump into my Land Rover and stopped at the double gate of the compound. It is wired on the inside. I stick my arms through the holes, trying to undo the ties when, to my right, something heavy hits the fence. The chain link bends, and a heavy body crashes through the bush.

"[Jules] comes to the gate, face glowing white in the African night. 'Are they gone?' he asks.

"'Who are they?'

"'The wild lions. They have been fighting with your cats for the last hour.'"[12]

We learned that these lions had terrorized the villagers by swooping down in raids and making off with horses and cattle. Trainers like Sylvester, Sled Reynolds, Annie Olivecrona (whom we called "Animal Annie"), and Steve Martin would team up on night watch to fend off the marauding lions. Even I was once shown who the boss was when our lioness walked past me and casually swatted me with her tail. I had a black-and-blue mark on my leg for about a week.

People who have traveled on airplanes with their pets know the drill: lead them into a small cage, say goodbye to them at the luggage counter, and wait for them to arrive on the baggage claim carousel after the flight. Some pet owners choose to sedate their pets. Professional animal handlers do not.

Animals are like people, one animal trainer explained, they adjust. There is a difference between *stress* and *distress*. Distress is when they are freaking out in the cargo hold, bellowing and roaring. Stress is when they are merely uncomfortable. We sent our movie zoo aboard the Lufthansa Combine which is half passengers and half cargo. The entire plane is pressurized, so the trainers could go back into the storage area to monitor and reassure the animals.

There was only one loss in transit: flamingos.

We flew a dozen of these elegant pink birds to Kenya. (No, they couldn't fly there on their own.) The reason we

---

12. Hubert Geza Wells, *Lights, Camera, Lions: Memoirs of a Real-Life Dr. Doolittle*, NY: Morgan James Publishing, 2017.

had to bring our own is that the Kenyan Wildlife Ministry had declared them a protected species and denied us permission to put their flamingos in the movie. We contracted with a professional game-catcher to provide them—in those days you could still be a game-catcher—and he loaded them on a plane in Los Angeles. They were to change flights in Frankfort and be loaded onto the flight for Nairobi, Kenya. The stopover was a scheduled ten hours out of a total of thirty hours in confinement. By the time they got to Nairobi and their cages were opened they were all dead. We were in shock. It took some time to untangle what must have happened. I was told that the cages were not wide enough for them to completely extend their wings, and they died. We were all devastated by the loss.

In addition to the sad fate of the birds, we still needed a flock of them to film three sequences. The first was the romantic setting in which Vic and Sheena get to know each other better. The second was the title sequence where Sheena rides on her Zebra along the shore. Both scenes were shot in Lake Nakuru where there are hundreds of thousands of flamingos feeding in the water. In order to make the birds take flight behind Sheena, we flew helicopters above them, out of camera range, and the *whup-whup* sound of the rotors made them take flight.

The third flamingo scene is the dramatic end of the second act in which Sheena, captured and taken aloft on a helicopter, piloted by Tim Ward-Booth, is to be pushed to her death in the great Zambuli Falls. Pretending that the "firebird" (copter) has given her a headache, she puts her hand to her forehead in the psychic process that summons animal help. Almost immediately, per the script, "Zillions of the gorgeous pink birds" start to rise, "skittering over the water now, taking off, rising in flocks."

With real-life Thompson's Falls below (the spot where Vic first saw Sheena) there are countless flamingos, "wings flapping, making time." In the script, the pilot "panicked, hits controls. Flailing pink wings. The courageous birds have actually flown into the [cockpit] through the open door! HUGE CRAZY CLOSE-UPS. SHRIEKING birds, flashing beaks, Zanda [the bad guy's bad girl] SCREAMING as she tries to protect eyes and face. A sharp beak jabs into the back of the Pilot's neck. With a YELL, he jerks the controls." Zanda falls out of the door and plummets to the falls, screaming. The copter sets down hard, the Pilot is thrown out, and Sheena and two flamingos hop out, unharmed. Not a single flamingo was harmed in those scenes.

"The climactic scene was very difficult," recalled screenwriter Lorenzo Semple, Jr. "Sheena was in [a helicopter] being taken by the villain, drop her in, out of the [copter]. As always in those movies he never does it. He talks about it. If he dropped her, actually, instead of talking about dropping her, it would come to a happier end. But anyway, while she's talking, she talks, she calls a bunch of flamingos who come and attack the [helicopter] in flight and get into the cabin and throw the villain out. That, in a sense, to me, made the movie worth making."[13]

The sequence was shot mostly on the ground, with the camera low and tilting up as prop men poked prop birds (and the occasional real one) at the actors in the cockpit of

---

13. Interviewed for "The Writer Speaks" by the Writers Guild Foundation, 2013.

the helicopter. With no reference but the sky, it looked as if the copter was flying. Finally, to show the copter crashing, we strung a cable across Thompson's Falls and sailed an old, full-sized, decommissioned copter to its fiery end.

Our animal trainers were the best in the business, but there was one beast they could not tame: zebras. Although zebras are the same genus as horses and look like them, they are not horses and cannot be broken without great effort. How, then, did Sheena ride a zebra?

She didn't. She rode a horse.

Three horses, actually.

We brought three gorgeous identical white steeds to Kenya, each knowing a different slate of tricks, and when any of them was needed as the Queen of the Jungle's royal mount, she went to hair and make-up—just like Tanya—to be clipped and painted (not like Tanya). This took a special animal painting department that used non-toxic, animal-safe colors that were washed off at the end of each day, re-applied each morning, and touched up as needed between takes because Tanya bravely rode bareback. Technically, the script specified a *zebroid*, which is a zebra crossed with another equine such as a horse or donkey. The painting job was very successful but the only thing that gives it up is that horses and zebras have different size ears.

"The woman who painted those horses was very talented," says trainer Jules Sylvester. "She painted those horses beautifully with Mexican hair dye. She painted every bloody stripe and it looks so good. But the ears betray them. The horses knew to do the stunts with [trainer] Sled Reynolds. Zebras can be trained, but they're a pain in the ass. You've got to remember that they're a wild animal. Even though they look like a horse and walk like a horse and talk like a horse, you go near a zebra it'll kick the shit out of you."

When we wrapped the picture, as with the rhino, we let the horses stay in Kenya.[14] After washing off the stripes, of course. The reason we left them in Africa is that the United States has a fear of horses bringing an African virus back to the States. The same thing happened to my wife, Ani, and me after the movie ended. We went to give blood in Los Angeles for a charity and were told that, because we had been in Africa, we could not donate for seven years. (We were fine.)

One of the discussions a lot of people are having today is whether an animal is better off wild or in captivity. There is no dispute that animals live longer in captivity than in the wild; the question becomes a matter of the quality of life.

Dropping a former captive animal into the wild poses problems. "The average life span of a lion in captivity is just over twenty years," says Jules Sylvester, one of our animal experts, who adds that a lion's lifespan is considerably shorter in the wild, "mainly from disease, hunters, and other lions." What about the growing animal rights movement that says animals should be freed?

"That's the thing," Sylvester says. "They should be free. Okay, where are you gonna put 'em? 'Well, they should be free in the forest.' Right. Okay, let me take you from New York and you go to the Maasai Mara. Have a good day! And that's what happens. They put them with other animals and

---

14. This was also to prevent the horses bringing back to America any bugs they may have picked up in Kenya.

they've been with two other animals their whole life, especially elephants. 'So lunch is not at 3, then? Are you gonna do my toenails? Who's that over there? Look at that big sonofabitch elephant.' 'What are *you* doing here?' 'I dunno, somebody just put me here.'

"People have an opinion. But just because you have an opinion, that doesn't make it right. Where are you going to put the lions? 'How about the Maasai Mara?' 'Do you know that the Maasai are killing them there because they're eating their cows?' "Or this: You have a tiger in Toronto and a tiger in Los Angeles. They're highly endangered. They're bred in captivity. I'd like to take my tiger to Toronto to breed him and make more tigers. 'That's against the Endangered Species Act, sir.' 'There's only two left in the world. I want to go and breed them.' 'That's illegal, sir.' 'How? There's only two left, you asshole.' 'Well, they shouldn't be bred in captivity!'"

Freeing captive animals is like deporting someone who has been raised in America to the land where his parents or grandparents came from. It's as cruel as separating Mexican and South American children from their parents in a political tug-of-war over immigration. These things need to be thought out. And even that doesn't always help when the answers are wrong.

My son Dory; my nieces Mayan and Gal; with local friends on safari

Tanya up a tree

Ashley Boone's first attempt at advertising art for *Sheena*, a concept that director John Guillermin rejected

The funny Donovan Scott played Fletch in the traditional role of the hero's best friend

Sheena (Tanya Roberts) comforts the dying Shaman
(Princess Elizabeth of Toro)

Our long-anticipated Telex from Coca-Cola topper Richard C. Gallop
congratulating John Guillermin and me and liking *Sheena*

Final display ad for the film following Guillermin's dictates

Animal handler Jules Sylvester and our Hollywood chimpanzees

The perfect Sheena (Tanya Roberts) innocently showers in a jungle waterfall

At the World Premiere of *Sheena*. L-R my son Dory, me, Changa, director John Guillermin, and exhibitor Henry Plitt

Sheena (Tanya Roberts) astride her horse that was painted to look like a zebra

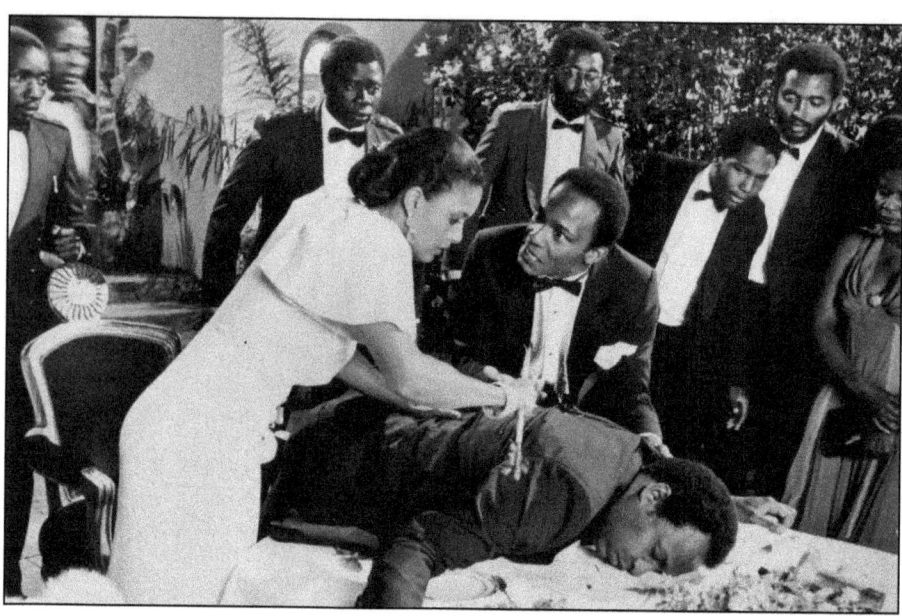

(L-R) Countess Zanda (France Zobda) and a worried Prince Otwani (Trevor Thomas) lean over the assassinated body of King Jabalani (Clifton Jones)

Vic (Ted Wass), Sheena (Tanya Roberts), and her pet chimp Changa at a lookout point watching for their pursuers

Tragedy Strikes

SOMETHING HAPPENED BEHIND the scenes while we were shooting the sequence in which Sheena and her elephant break the Shaman out of jail. On the night of Saturday, March 24, we were shooting in Karura Forest. The crew had flipped their hours so that they slept during the day and shot all night. There was a huge tent that had been erected as our location office. I was watching John set up a complicated sequence involving the actors and the elephant when I was called away unexpectedly for a phone call. Remember, this was years before cell phones and our only means of outside contact, especially far away from Nairobi on location in Karura, was by shortwave radio. I went to the tent and it was from Guy McElwaine back at the studio.

The signal was scratchy and weak but I heard Guy's voice, "Yoram, I have some bad news. John's son, Michael, was killed a few hours ago in a car accident in Lake Tahoe."

This hit me hard. Michael had just left Kenya, where he was working under logistics manager Danny Ben Menahem in the film's motor pool. He was going home to see his dentist back in the States.

I knew that John and Michael were not especially close; John had been treating Michael harshly before the young man's departure. The news was devastating, but not as devastating as what Guy told me next.

"He'll probably want to go home," he said, and I agreed. But then he added, "I'll send you quickly another director to finish the film." He was thinking that this would be the way to solve our problem of being over budget and behind schedule.

I was shocked. I couldn't believe what I heard from Guy. Would the studio actually use the death of a man's son as an excuse to pull the rug out from under him? The worst tragedy that can befall any parent is the loss of a child. Taking him off the film would surely kill him. I had heard this kind of callous Hollywood story before, but I never thought I would find myself in the middle of one.

"Don't worry about it," I said, searching for a solution. "We can talk about it later because I think I know how to solve the problem." I kept looking for words that would make the studio head back off. "I'll have Max Kleven (stunt unit director and a DGA member) take over for a few days until John comes back from the funeral." This seemed to mollify Guy and we hung up.

I went slowly back to the set hoping I could think of how to handle this. How could I break the news to John with so many people around? Should I let him continue shooting, or would that seem trivial, if not cruel, considering what I knew. In the distance I could see him confidently settling everyone into place and calling "action" for the elephant to break the jail fence. He had no way of knowing that I was about to tell him something that would change his life forever.

But when? I decided to wait until he had finished the shot, but not to break the news to him there on the set. I wanted to get him away from all these other people to accord him privacy when I told him the news.

I took his friend, associate producer Christian Ferry, aside and told him to wrap at 2 a.m. and send them to lunch. ("Lunch" is in the middle of the night on a night shoot.) When John said "cut" I went to him and said, "Come, John, I need you to go with me in the car back to Nairobi."

He said, "Yoram, if you want to tell me that I'm fired, that's okay; you can tell it to me here. I'm used to it."

"No, John, I have to talk to you at the hotel. Please don't give me any trouble. Let's get into the car."

This seemed to confuse him. His eyes betrayed curiosity, but I said nothing.

"Then tell me what's going on."

I said, "Only when we get to the hotel."

We drove in absolute silence to Nairobi. I hoped that, by the time we got to the Norfolk, I would think of a way to tell him what I knew. Every minute felt like an hour. By 3 a.m. we were at the hotel and John unlocked his bungalow. I followed him inside when, at the entrance to his suite, he grasped my left arm. "I know you want to tell me I'm fired," he said. "Don't worry. I've been fired off other pictures and survived." He started to become arrogant but I stayed serious.

"No John," I said grimly. "It's worse than that. It's about Mike. It's bad news."

"What is it?"

"Michael is dead. He was killed in a car accident tonight in Lake Tahoe."

The words struck him like a spear in the heart. He said nothing, but collapsed onto my shoulders like he fell from the rooftop of a ten-story building. Suddenly he was no longer this arrogant son-of-a-bitch. He dug his head into my shoulder and started to cry like a little boy. I never knew the guy had any tears in his body. Then he pulled away and started hitting the wall of the bungalow. He hit it again and again, still sobbing, only now his sobs were yells of frustration and grief. Here was a father who had neglected his son, and now his son was gone.

I stayed with him while he calmed down enough to think more clearly. We made plans for him to get back to the States with Christian Ferry as soon as they could get transportation out. Max took over while John went home to be with his son.

He returned four days later a changed man. "He was like a little child," recalls Richard Hartley, who composed the score for the movie and was a friend of both John and Michael. "He was broken. Because I was friendly with his son when we were in Nairobi, we were similar age, after he died I got the impression that John thought of me as a second son. It's strange for me to say that, but his personality completely changed and he was much more mild." He recalls Michael as, "a completely different kind of person than John. He was a very gentle, very sweet boy where his father was very abrasive. After that happened, it was a completely different experience for John. Michael was not like his father at all. He didn't talk about his father and he didn't talk about his family. It was very sad. When someone close to you dies it takes a long, long time to get over it."

Adds Donovan Scott, "That was a pretty terrible thing, and it happened close to the end. I'd say we had a couple of weeks, a month at the most left of shooting. He was just very serious. He wasn't joking much anymore. He just got down to brass tacks and shot the scenes. Nothing was very complicated after that, because he'd had some complicated scenes, but he simplified things. You couldn't tell anything had happened except John wasn't 'there.' It was just terrible because I had met his son on the set. He actually worked on the film for a while. We became friends. I had some footage on him that I sent to John.[15] He was doing odds and ends."

John was beaten but not broken. After two weeks he managed to summon the bravado to continue, but anyone who knew him before, as I did, could see that he would never be the same again.

---

15. Donovan shot home video footage throughout the production.

Dances With Composers

JOHN'S PENCHANT FOR AUTHENTICITY drove the company to extraordinary efforts, some of which showed up on the screen and others of which did not. One of the most unusual stories behind the scenes of *Sheena* involved finding dancers to perform the Zambuli "healing earth" ritual that begins and ends the film. You might think that Africa was up to here with dancers, given how many past movies set there have shown natives performing tribal rituals. The stereotype persists, and we wanted to avoid it when we went in search of dancers to appear in our film.

The healing earth ceremony was a key plot point: a man whose skin is covered in tumors is buried up to his neck in the ground while dancers in colorful garb and animal masks perform around him. From the script (scenes 4-7):

> *The forest around them coming alive with bonfires. The drums grow louder. Starting to dance by the leaping flames, their faces wonderfully painted. Tribesmen have dug into that patch of loam around the Buried Man. Strong arms have grasped him, he is suddenly*

pulled from the earth. His skin is absolutely clear and healthy. Not a trace of those tumors we heard about. He lifts his hands to the sky and slowly turns, exhibiting himself. Healed.

The second scene with the dancers occurs at the end of the film and is a repeat of the first except, this time, Vic Casey is the wounded man who is being healed by the sacred ground.

There are lots of dancers in Kenya, but for John Guillemin none of them was what he wanted. John and I must have gone to ten auditions in Nairobi. To all of them, John said, "They don't look African enough." What he meant was that they looked too "modern."

To our good fortune and luck, Les Ballets Africains came to Kenya from Guinea to perform at a party for Kenyan Independence Day, December 12, 1983. By coincidence, I was at Nairobi Airport picking up Columbia Pictures production executive Gary Martin when I saw them arriving as a group. They looked as if they were from another world, a poor world, and they brought with them strange and ancient musical instruments. Knowing that we still lacked a dancing troupe, I approached them and invited them to audition for Guillermin and me at the hotel.

Guillermin was enchanted when he saw them. By then they had changed their travel clothes into their traditional performance costumes, which were almost topless, including the women. Strong and exciting African music hit the dining room where they were auditioning. I never saw, in my life, people jumping higher than Baryshnikov, but these immensely talented performers did and made it look just as effortless. After the dance, I did not hesitate to summon their representatives to my office in the hotel to offer them a contract.

Three people arrived. As the troupe was from Guinea, which was a Communist country, the troika of representatives who showed up were practiced in the technique of divide-and-conquer (how they could divide me, let alone conquer me, is a question I don't know how to answer). Each of them had a separate role in our negotiations. First there was a Politruk whose job was to indoctrinate the dancers in Communism with an hour-long lecture every day. He was dressed in a military uniform in the mold of Fidel Castro. Next there was a company manager who was in charge of all the administrative functions. Finally there was the choreographer and artistic director, Italo Zambo.

In the meeting, I offered each of the men $10,000 under the table to sign a contract for their troupe to appear in the movie. They said that I was short $10,000. When I asked who the mystery $10,000 was for, they said it was for Ahmed Sékou Touré, the President of Guinea. Because Les Ballets Africains was the country's chief export, Sékou Touré had put himself in full control of them and their business affairs.

Everything was set; they would wrap their Kenyan New Year's engagement, return to Guinea, and then come back to Kenya in a month to film their scenes for *Sheena*. In the meantime, I would send composer Richard Hartley to Conakry, the capitol of Guinea, to work with them on the dance and to compose original music for it. Hartley, then

37, who had played in the band and was the arranger for *The Rocky Horror Show*, was just beginning a long and productive composing career. He went to Guinea expecting to spend a few days getting down to business. He soon found himself hostage in a political power play.

"You sent me to Guinea," Hartley tells me all these years later, "but you didn't give me a visa. In those days there was Pan-Am One (Pan-American Airlines flight #1) that used to go around the world anti-clockwise, and that's what I went on. I had to change planes in Sierra Leone and, because the plane was delayed, the guys from Les Ballets Africains were supposed to meet me but they waited and waited and I didn't come, so when I arrived I had no visa and I had to bribe the guys at Immigration $20 to get in. Then I got a taxi and I didn't have a precise address but I knew roughly, I'd got a name of the building. But there are no street signs in Guinea, it's 'the blue house by the three palm trees.' I asked the taxi driver, 'How much?' He said, 'It could be ten dollars.' I said fine. We're driving around and I turn around and suddenly he's driving against the traffic. I said, 'What are you doing?' He said, 'It could be *twenty* dollars.' That's why he did it—to scare me so he could get more money out of me."

It also happened to be New Year's Eve. After Richard checked into his hotel, the Minister of Culture came to see him.

"It's a Muslim country and they don't drink," Richard continues, "except on New Year's Eve. He came and he was drunk. He was very nice, but then he said to me, 'Did you bring my present? My New Year's present?' I thought he was joking. I said, 'blah blah blah' but he kept saying about this present. He had these guys in a Jeep. He clapped his hands and they came in with machine guns and I realized he wasn't joking. I said, 'Oh, yeah, yeah, yeah.' So I go to my room and, fortunately, you had given me some of Columbia's money, so I gave him $100 which is, you know, a lot of money to him. He was very happy."

Not knowing what Richard was going through in Guinea, we continued blissfully shooting the film in Kenya. After several days, however, I had not heard from him. Reaching him by phone was not possible, and I started to worry. Guinea was in West Africa, 3300 miles away and Guinea, as a Communist country, did not make communication easy. I was afraid Richard was dead. Finally a shortwave radio operator in London reached me and connected me with him. As soon as we were talking, he begged me to get him out of Guinea. As he told me his horror story, I was praying that we would not lose our shortwave connection before I could find a way to get him out.

Later I learned what had happened. With Richard booked into the hotel, various people from the ballet started drinking in the hotel bar and signing the tab to Richard's room. And they didn't even invite him. Moreover, they kept him there until his visa expired and his return plane ticket ran out.

By this time, the Guinean Cultural Minister had taken over and sent word to me that he would not allow the troupe to come to Kenya as promised unless he was paid more money. This news was a disaster. I told John about it and I knew it would be a disaster for him, too, so I started to look for somebody to fly to Conakry to rescue Richard and to bring the dancers to location. After a couple of days, I found an American lady named "Sandy" (not her real name). When we met in Nairobi, I saw that she had a look of Mata Hari combined with Indiana Jones. She was an attractive blonde with blue eyes, was tall, and spoke in a Southern accent. Her dialogue, and the way she spoke it to me, seemed straight out of a spy movie.

"What is the mission?" she asked.

"Bring Richard back, and the dancers. I need them all here in a week to shoot, by hook or by crook." I gave her 42 airline tickets and an advance of $1,000 on a $2,000 fee, and she said, "Well done." I swear I am not making this up.

Three days later, I went to Nairobi Airport. I had special permits to wait on the tarmac. The plane landed and, when its door opened, Sandy was the first one to come out. She approached me and, in an adventurer's voice, said, "Yoram, mission completed." I hugged her and I noticed that the Politruk was not in the group. I asked Sandy where he was. "He was killed in a car accident," she said, "this is his replacement, the Minister of Culture, and with him you must speak." Then Richard came down the airplane stairs and I hugged him. Behind them was the Minister of Culture of Guinea (who looked a bit like Idi Amin) and the rest of the group. "Watch out for the Minister of Culture," Sandy confided quietly, "he is a tricky person." I took this very seriously as I shook his hand. He said, "Nice to meet you," and coughed. Being a hypochondriac, I noticed his cough immediately and got an idea. I said to him, "It looks like you're not feeling well."

He said, "You're right."

I said, "Don't worry, let's get into my car and I'll take you to the city hospital of Nairobi. A friend of mine, Dr. Silverstein, will take care of you."

I walked the Minister into the hospital and told Dr. Silverstein to take care of him. The doctor understood what I meant by "take care of him." The Minister got a nice room for himself and I took Dr. Silverstein aside and told him in a low voice, "Don't release this man until I tell you." Silverstein didn't ask why. I went into the Minister's room and said to him, "I heard that you are not going to perform in the movie unless you get more money. What happened to the man I made the original deal with?" The Minister told me that he had been killed in an accident. I tried to be diplomatic and still make my point. "You are my honored guest, but if you change the contract with me that you have signed, you are only getting out of this hospital in a coffin." To my surprise, he smiled and said, "Okay, how about compensating us with liquor and cigarettes?" I smiled back and agreed. But I didn't shake his hand.

Now the dancers' story gets even stranger. Two days later, at four o'clock in the morning, the troupe boards an old Kenyan bus driven by a local driver. They have all their props, costumes, and instruments and they're heading for a place called South Hell's Gate where we were going to film them. It was a drive of some 120 kilometers which would take more than three hours over rough roads. As usual, Guillermin and I used our French helicopter to get to the location first. Time went by and the troupe didn't show up. Finally one of the people in the transportation department arrived and said he saw some people who looked like dancers on the side of a road near some kind of accident. Immediately I instructed the French pilot to take off with me to track the route that the bus was supposed to take.

Reaching the spot by air, I was stunned. We found the bus, but it was not on the road. It had gone down a sheer cliff and was balanced precariously on a huge tree that was growing out of the rocks not far from the top edge. Had the tree not been there, the bus would have plummeted a thousand feet into the chasm. By this time, some of the dancers had managed to climb up the rocks to safety and were sitting in shock on the side of the road. Others were still making their way up the stone façade. By amazing coincidence, the accident had taken place across the road from an Italian convent and a contingent of nuns was ministering to the injured. I had my pilot set me down on the road so I could check on them. Fortunately, nobody had been killed, but they were all terribly shaken. Once I confirmed that they would be all right, I had the helicopter take me back to location where I told Guillermin what had happened and said that he would have to shoot other material until the group recovered. I also sent a vehicle to collect the dancers and bring them back to their hotel. Two days later, when they did perform, some of them still had bandages under their costumes.

I still marvel that nobody was killed or seriously injured, and that a single African tree happened to be growing from the cliff at that exact spot and had caught the bus as though it was the hand of God. Not only that, but that the whole thing took place across the road from a convent of nuns. I know that Communists aren't supposed to believe in God, but, after this, I like to think that the church door was open in case they thought about entering.

With the blessing of hindsight, Richard could look back somewhat fondly on his African gambit. "As you can imagine," he says, "that New Year's Eve was frightening. The guys who ran the ballet company didn't say anything, They were all completely brainwashed and terrified. The other thing was, they were the jewel in the crown of the country. They were a very useful item to send around the world as an ambassador to the doctrine of the country. They weren't stupid enough to upset the cash cow. I remember, a few years later, they came to London and were dancing at the Palladium. They were very well paid."

As for the music that Richard was supposed to compose in Guinea, he says, "What John didn't tell me was that he wanted that piece he saw them do in Nairobi, the one at the audition you described. But they were under the impression that he wanted a whole different thing. If he'd told me that then, it would have been easier. They wanted to do something completely different than what they were renowned for, which was very sexy African tribal dancing, and so we spent two days doing something that was completely inappropriate, and that's why, when they came back, John said, 'No, no, I don't like that. Remember that piece you did before?' That's what happened. Then it was modified. We recorded the drums live at midnight one night on the set out in the Rift Valley. That's the story."

But not entirely, because reminiscing about it in the cafeteria after John and I got back to Columbia and the picture was being edited, I said to John, "Imagine if we had hired Paul McCartney to do the music and he had been a hostage in Guinea?" Neither of us dared think of an answer.

Besides, Richard Hartley's score for *Sheena* is breathtaking. It captures the sweep of the African scenery, the intimacy of the love story, and the excitement of all the action. His music for Les Ballets Africains sounds like authentic African music. I wouldn't have had it any other way. Whether Richard would agree is another matter.

By the way, if you wonder, this whole *mishegoss* that cost me nights of not sleeping and Columbia hundreds of thousands of dollars lasted maybe two minutes in the final film, at night, when you can barely see them. We could easily have used local Kenyan dancers. This shows the power a director has once a film is in production. I was held hostage by John's imagination.

Behind the Camera

SHEENA ENJOYED THE TALENTS of so many people from so many different cultures working together that a day on the set must have sounded like building on the Tower of Babel (before the scattering). For the most part, the English, Italian, American, African, and Israeli crew members got along, despite the weather—hot one day, rainy another—and the sheer amount of work they had to do.

A movie as big and complex as *Sheena* hired a number of people from outside Kenya because, at the time, Kenya's film industry was just getting started. Indeed, thanks to the experience they gained working on our film, many Kenyans went on to make movies and TV shows in their home country after we left. Our crew roster included not only animal handlers but assistant directors, electricians, builders, pyrotechnic experts, helicopter pilots, special effects riggers, camera crews, costumers, and remarkably resourceful prop masters.

The team also included its share of egos and, regrettably, one that smacked of racism.

It started during lunch on location in Hell's Gate where everyone was standing in the catering line. By tradition, the actors get to go first because they may need to study their lines or get their make-up touched up. (Our actors often chose to wait in line like everyone else.) Suddenly Tim Ward-Booth, one of our helicopter pilots and an ex-RAF flyer, cut ahead of everyone else. When the man who was behind him complained, Tim told him to "fuck off". This created an incident because Tim was white and the men in front of whom he cut were black. The men came to me and said, "Yoram, we're going home" and told me what had just happened. I walked quickly over to Tim, hoping that a solution would come into my mind before I got there.

It did. I realized that this was not a racial divide, it was a status issue, a product of the English class system.

"Look, Tim," I said, "that's not okay what you did." Meanwhile, the man he stepped in front of was standing beside me waiting for me to do something. In desperation, I said, "Can the two of you make peace?"

Both men shook their heads "No." Then I had an idea. I asked the crew member, "Did you ever ride in a helicopter?"

I could see that Tim knew where I was going and had begun to smile.

"No," the crew member said. He knew that helicopter rides were considered a privilege.

"Okay, Tim," I said, "forget about lunch. You take him up for ten minutes and enjoy Africa from the air. Give him a good time."

Tim agreed and he and the man he'd insulted took off. After ten minutes they hadn't returned. Nor after fifteen. I started to wonder whether the men would become friends or resume their feud and Tim would push the man out of the 'copter. I needn't have been concerned. When they set down on the ground, both of them stepped out of the cockpit smiling and shaking hands. While they were aloft alone, the two of them simply began relating to each other as people regardless of class.

I often wished that all of society's differences could be settled so easily.

There was, however, a tinge of racism that showed itself in a way I never expected; that is, between the African-Americans and the Africans. The African-American members of the crew were very much American despite having their roots, however far back, in Africa. They tended to place themselves above the indigenous African crew members in the same way that American tourists often condescend to, or dismiss, the residents of foreign lands they visit. It also, regrettably, applied to whites. This came to an ugly head on the night of April 13 when a fight broke out in the bar of the Norfolk Hotel between Charles Allen, a musician and the leader of the Epistrophe Quartet, and five white stunt performers, some of whom had played mercenaries in the film. According to reports, a man walked up to a white British woman married to a black Kenyan and insulted her. Somehow Allen, who headed the Music Department at Nairobi's St. Mary's school, became involved in the melee. The next day he identified his assailant, who was taken to the police station.[16] It was a private wrap party, but as Executive Producer I was dragged into doing damage control when the *Kenya Times* editorialized about it and insinuated that we were a company of racists. My public statement on behalf of the company said:

> *On behalf of Colgems Productions Limited, the cast and crew of 'SHEENA', I am appalled and greatly upset by the incident that took place at the Norfolk Hotel after the farewell party on Friday 13 April. However, we must stress that the party was a private affair given in appreciation of the contribution of many people, both black and white, local and foreign, to the production of 'SHEENA' in Kenya.*
>
> *Whatever happened involving various individual[s] was an entirely separate and private matter which should be handled by the police. I advise anyone who has any complaints regarding this incident to pursue that matter through the Kenyan police authorities and the laws of Kenya and the aggressors should be punished.*
>
> *This incident [has] nothing to do with Colgems Productions or Columbia Pictures and I deeply resent any attempt to link either Company with derogatory racial opinions or attitudes as I am a firm believer in equal rights and non-discrimination and this was our practice both officially and unofficially throughout our time in Kenya.*

---

16. "Police 'Net Film Actor," by Mitch Odero and Margaretta wa Gacheru, *Kenya Times*, April 18, 1984.

Our legal representatives prepared contingency defense scenarios and made it clear that Mr. Allen was not our employee and that those involved in the fight were separate contractors. In addition, the Kenya Film Crew Association came to our defense. (In fact, their General Secretary Joe S. Yambo later praised us for hiring four of their stuntmen.) There was a brief exchange of posturing letters but, if any legal action ever commenced, it did not involve us and I never heard of it.

* * *

Coca-Cola may have wanted to thaw its frozen assets in Kenya, but that doesn't mean we were allowed to spend them without proper paperwork. The problem was that we had to make disbursements in a country that didn't use employee W-2 forms and whose people didn't have bank accounts. Traditional payroll services would be useless. Moreover, Kenyan extras and workers expected to be paid in cash, not checks. Half of my dealings were in cash, and half of those were under the table. Who can ask for receipts for such things? But since we had to appease Coke's and Columbia's accounting departments, this took some imagination.

The issue was made clear to a Coke accountant who showed up one day to check the books. Ed Stefanovich acted like a sales agent counting a grocer's inventory (perhaps because Coca-Cola dealt with so many grocers, he thought I was one). He was puzzled when he looked at the pay roster; all he saw was a string of thumb prints. That was how the Samburu and Maasai tribe members signed for their pay. How can you get signed receipts from three hundred black tribesmen, without IDs, who sign with the ends of their fingers, and you have to pay them separately, because if you do not, no one will get anything because the chief will take everything for himself? The only solution was to have each person "sign" for him or herself, and then go away paid. When the studio accountant questioned the process, I told him, "Don't make me laugh. Look, you're here on an organized three-day safari. Why don't you relax and enjoy yourself. Then you can go home and tell everybody that you had a great time in Kenya." Before he had time to think about it, I added, "If not, you can stay here and make the movie yourself." That did it. He never bothered us again.[17]

* * *

I used my executive producer status to become an African Robin Hood. I raised crew salaries, provided extra food, and even paid to build an irrigation system so the Maasai living in Hell's Gate could have drinking water, water for their sheep, and for their crops. So what if Coca-Cola had to sell a few more cans; the frozen money had to be used there anyway, right?

We were also pleased to donate 400,000 Kenyan shillings to the Armed Forces Central Services Fund for, as Chief of General Staff General I. K. Mulinge announced at the February 21 ceremony, the welfare of the members of the armed forces. The donations, of course, came from our budget.

---

17. There was some talk after we wrapped that some local hires had been cheated by the contracting agents we had engaged to hire them. They were private contractors not associated with Colgems. Nevertheless, we extended our insurance policies to cover them in case of injury.

We were under the protection of the Kenyan Army.[18] This was as much for President Moi's safety as ours, as there was the always-present danger of rebel attack and security officials wanted to make sure that actual guns were not being imported along with our prop guns. The same concern held for the many trucks and other vehicles we used. Everything had to be accounted for, and special permission had to be obtained even to drive our trucks (called lorries) at night, so concerned was the Kenyan government about dissidents.

* * *

One morning something was missing. Something big. Namely, the Kenyan Army Orchestra who were supposed to be welcoming Vic and Fletch at the airport. I had hired them through the Kenyan Chief of Staff and they were to have been at the airport for a 6 A.M. call. When they were not, I called the Chief of Staff (for whom I had built, out of our budget, a fence for his horse farm) and yelled, "General Musamba, where is your band?" He woke up instantly and assured me he would find them. He drove around the streets of Nairobi as the sun came up looking for them, and when he found them—he never told me where—got them to show up two hours later so we could shoot.

Minor glitches like that aside, we enjoyed extraordinary cooperation with the Kenyan government. I cannot begin to imagine how much we saved—several millions of dollars, I am sure—by making that donation to the Kenyan Army who supplied us with all the trucks and soldiers and

---

18. A confidential letter of agreement was given to Associate Producer Christian Ferry by S.M. Muio, Administration Police Commandant to the Office of the President.

protection that we needed. This is why I was surprised when two men appeared one morning when we were preparing to shoot the assassination scene saying that they were from the Kenyan Tax Department. They were well-dressed in jackets and ties and looked eminently presentable, just like real bureaucrats. They told a crew member that they were looking for "the person in charge" so I was summoned immediately.

When I caught my first sight of them, they were checking out every aspect of the scene and my crew, and were helping themselves to coffee at our catering wagon. Suspecting a shakedown (because we had already contracted with the appropriate government agencies), I decided to make the first move. In a loud voice, I asked the person who had fetched me, "What are these two actors doing at the coffee machine? Why are they not in their place and ready for the scene you're supposed to be shooting?"

They heard me as the crew member looked confused and stammered, "But Yoram, these men are not actors, they're from the Kenyan Tax Department."

"Are you serious?" I pretended. "I thought they were actors. They look like actors. In fact, they look like movie stars." Obviously I knew that they weren't but I had an idea of how to throw them off. "No, no," one of them said, "we're from the Kenyan Tax Department." Without reacting to what they said, I kept on the offensive, telling them, "Oh come on, you're actors! Go into the costume caravan and tell them I said you should be dressed in wardrobe for the scene we're about to shoot." Then I lowered my voice and pretended to take them into my confidence: "We invested a lot of money in Kenya for this film, and I would be very grateful if you would be photographed instead of arguing with me."

They looked at each other. The idea of being in a movie did not seem so bad to them. "Yes," they replied together. I stuck them in a scene with hundreds of other extras and they were lost in the crowd. More importantly, they completely forgot that they had come to shake us down.

* * *

In Kenya as in Hollywood it is not unusual for a producer to hire friends and family members for the crew, usually in minor positions where they can't get into trouble or slow things down. Sometimes this is called "nepotism," but I like to think of it as a return favor. For example, after I worked out an agreement with the Minister of Tourism, he asked me out of the blue if I would be interested in being a go-between between him and Israel to sell them 80,000 chicken eggs from his farm. Of course, I had to say yes (I didn't wind up doing it). Another time, Daniel Sindiyo, who arranged for us to have access to Kenya's game preserves, asked me if I could find a job for his 18-year-old son, David, on our crew. In this case, I said yes. I shouldn't have.

I seconded David to our driving unit, which had just taken delivery of a beautiful, brand new Mercedes tanker that would be used to bring fuel to our vehicles on distant locations because there were no gas stations where we were going. It was a full tanker waiting not far from our set where Guillermin was shooting a scene. Most of the crew was there. It was a terribly hot day and there were probably petrol fumes floating around the tanker. Not thinking how dangerous it was, David lit up a cigarette. Suddenly in the distance I heard a BOOM! and turned to see pieces of metal hitting the ground from what had been that brand-new Mercedes tanker. Luckily no one, including David, was hurt, but this could have been a deadly disaster. Fortunately, the insurance company bought a brand-new tanker for the Kenyan army. David was assigned elsewhere after that.

* * *

It's a producer's job to see that the production runs smoothly, and that was put in jeopardy three months before the shoot when members of the English construction crew came to me complaining about working conditions. From my experience, I knew right away that they weren't really complaining about conditions, they were using that as a wedge to get more money. They had already been making small requests for salary increases beyond what we had agreed upon. They were being paid, housed, fed, and given per diem. I knew it was coming to a head.

It happened late one night after many of them had been partying at Florida 2000, not only drinking but dallying with some of the women who earned a living "entertaining" mzungus.

"We can't work in these conditions," their representative told me. "The acacia trees have sharp needles that stick us." They wanted boots, they wanted this, they wanted that—even though they were experienced and had been told, before they left for Africa, what they would be required to do. It was a shakedown. These were excellent builders and it would be hard to lose them, but I had no choice. I went to the production office, took out all fifteen of their passports, and bought fifteen tickets back to London.

After I fired everyone and gave them their papers and tickets, "Jimmy" (not his real name) took my arm and pulled me aside. "You can't send me home," he pleaded.

"I'm sorry to lose you," I said, "but you stood with the others."

"No, no, that isn't what I mean," he said. "I have no problem with the dismissal, but I cannot go back to my wife." He sounded genuinely afraid.

"What's the deal?" I asked.

He blushed. "I got gonorrhea from one of the girls at the club."

"That's your problem," I said.

He walked toward me, lowering his head. "When a man has been on location for months, the first thing his wife expects him to do once he gets home is go to bed with her. If I can't do it because I picked something up in Africa, it will end my marriage. Please, let me stay for a few more days, until this thing passes, and then I'll go away. I give you my word I'll go."

I did, and so did he.

* * *

It drives studio executives crazy when they have a production shooting on a distant location, far away from their supervision and sometimes in areas so remote that telephone contact is impossible. At the same time, filmmakers love being on distant locations for exactly the same reasons. The studios have ways of dealing with this: they plant a company spy among the crew (we found out who ours was early on), they send emissaries to location (not a problem), and they bombard the producer with telexes (the precursor to faxes and e-mails) demanding daily updates. All of these, of course, take time away from the job at hand, which is making the movie.

Six weeks into *Sheena*, I had to calm the concerns of Guy McElwaine, Shel Shrager, Tom MacCarthy (post-production), and Gary Martin (operations) who wanted to know how the film was going. (From the tone of their telex, they actually wanted to know how the *hell* the film was going.) They had heard about the dancers' bus going off the cliff and various grumblings from the crew, and they wanted to know the score from 9,500 miles away.

"This is not the time to make panic decisions and psychological mistakes that could jeopardize the completion and delivery of the picture," I wired back to them on January 30, 1984. "Believe me that in the given circumstances I am running the picture in the best possible way and that my attitude is to fully support and encourage the director, cast and crew who are fighting an extremely tough location picture. During the past two weeks we have shot to schedule despite the traffic accident to dancers, illness, escape of wild animals, etc. In order to try and bring the picture in on time here are some suggestions arrived at after discussion with Ray Lovejoy (editor), John Guillermin, etc."

I listed a number of things that could speed things up and not hurt the film including combining locations, letting second or third units handle certain sequences with the main actors, and increasing the travel budget so crew members could fly between distant locations instead of taking buses. Regarding the crew, I said I would "re-evaluate situation with some crew members so that the tired and sick who have cracked and who are slowing production can be replaced with new and fresh personnel. This will not affect schedule."

I assured McElwaine—but mostly Shel, Tom, and Gary who were more familiar with the intricacies of editing and post-production—that we were supplying them with copious notes so that the film could be put together quickly and efficiently. I was forced to note that "there are no facilities in Nairobi for mixing down 35mm tracks" and requested a sound maintenance engineer be sent from the U.K. to set up a basic mixing console. Moving the heavy Steenbeck editing console from location to location was like hauling around a grand piano in a pickup truck, a gambit that demanded expensive recalibration at every new venue.

It must have worked because there was no more panic.

* * *

We had remarkably few injuries in the course of production, which is an extraordinary record for an action picture working with animals, many of them wild. When we did have the rare injury, it was usually the fault of a human, not an animal. Case in point: a Kikuyu tribesman who was the night watchman for our compound in Karen. While I was away at dinner one night, this fellow decided to get drunk and invite his girlfriend to see where he worked. He had been telling everybody "all these animals are my friends" but he obviously didn't bring the animals themselves into the loop. He started by stroking Big H, the rhino, who was used to human contact and ignored him. He worked his way to Magoo, the leopard, bragging, "All the animals love me, especially this one." To prove Magoo's affection, the man stuck his finger into the cage. Without another word, the leopard growled and bit off the man's finger.

Only when I got back from dinner did I hear about it. The next day the poor man had sobered up and was walking around with a huge bandage on his hand, minus one finger. "The leopard took my finger. The leopard is a cannibal."

I gave him sympathy but told him, "You should have stuck your finger in your ass instead of a leopard's mouth."

* * *

South Hell's Gate National Park in Naivasha was seventy-six miles from Nairobi, a drive of nearly three hours over rough roads, but that was where John wanted to film the opening scene in which young Sheena's parents are killed in a cave-in while searching for the legendary healing earth of "Gudjara Mountain." Our location recce found an opening on the side of a cliff that could serve as the cave, but it happened to be a considerable height off the ground. In order to film the Ameses entering and the newly orphaned Janet/Sheena escaping as dust threatens to engulf her, we built a ramp from ground level to the opening some thirty feet up, and then covered it with red-brown soil to look like the surrounding land.

EXT. CAVEMOUTH - DAWN

> Janet comes running by, stops as she sees something... The child goes warily into the cavemouth. She calls for her mother. Her mother turns and shouts a warning to go. The cry echoes and echoes. But an amazing thing happens. Instead of diminishing with each repetition, the echo becomes louder and louder. The sound is terrifying and demonic, a great chunk of rock falls. Janet stands paralyzed, holding her ears. The whole earth is rumbling.

John brought out every moment of danger and tension in the sequence, showing the parents crawling toward the cave exit and almost making it before being covered by a sudden rock fall.

Dust billows out of the cave enfolding itself around the little girl. As she steps from the cloud, she sees the Shaman and a group of Zambulis staring at her in awe. The Shaman kneels before her and takes her by the shoulders:

> SHAMAN
> The prophesy has come to pass. On a day when the sacred mountain cries out, a golden girl-child will come from the depths of Gudjara! And she shall grow in wisdom and be the protector of the Zambuli and all their creatures. And she shall be called by the name of Sheena. ... Queen of the jungle!

* * *

Hell's Gate National Park was a pathway for early humans into the Rift Valley, which is known as "the navel of Mankind," for this is where fossil discoveries have been made that trace the origin of homo sapiens. A fairly small park compared with others in Africa, it is nevertheless the home for lions, cheetahs, and leopards, but it mostly known as the home of the rare Lammergeyer vultures and other birds.

It is primarily a Maasai region (the Maasai Cultural Center is located there) as well as a camping area. There are presently some forty-two separate tribes that are recognized by the Kenyan government and a few more that are not, with the possible number exceeding fifty. Among the seventeen tribes with whom we had the honor of working, most of our dealings were with the Kikuyu, Maasai, and Samburu. The tribe in our film were the fictional Zambulis who were played on screen by an assortment of players from all the Kenyan tribes. Fortunately, they arrived wearing their own traditional tribal dress, saving us enormous time and expense in costuming. This was typical of the co-operation we enjoyed from the Kenyan people.

* * *

The image that many people still carry of Sheena (if poster sales and Google Images are any indication) are Tanya's two nude scenes. The first occurs early in the film—scene 37, to be precise—and was shot at Queens Cave in Aberdare Park.

> *Full on Sheena, innocently naked, shielded just enough by a prismatic spray as she bathes in the falls. Flash*

of her body, she's dived off a rock into the pool, she's swimming toward where her scanty costume hangs on a bush.

It lasts all of seventeen seconds, mostly in extreme long shot but, combined with another nude scene, would set the stage for a ratings flap just before the film was to be released.

Scene 91, also set in Aberdare National Park, occurs after Sheena and Vic have eluded the mercenaries and have spent a chaste night sleeping beneath a tree under the chaperoning eyes of the chimpanzee Chim. The next morning, as Vic, sitting beside a pond, fully clothed, brushes his teeth with a stick, his jaw drops as Sheena casually breezes past him, completely naked, and begins bathing in the pond. "Vic's mind isn't exactly on his teeth," the script reads. "He reacts, catching his breath."

"Why don't you come in and wash?" she asks guilelessly. "You're dirty as a wart hog."

Perhaps channeling what bashful members of the audience may be thinking, Vic says, "No, I don't think so."

"Water frightens you?"

"Not exactly."

Nevertheless, she goads him to join her, commenting on his dress shirt and necktie, "From what animals do those come?"

"The wild silk moth," Vic answers, "It roams in Bloomingdale's." Ted's deadpan delivery perfectly contrasts with Tanya's innocent query. And *innocent* is the word that makes both the waterfall and pond scenes inoffensive, even chaste, despite the display of Tanya's considerable assets.

What made it work?

In the story, Sheena was bathing nude in the stream because that's the only source of water. It's played for innocence and that's how it was shot. The thing is, when you see a body like hers, it's hard to be naive. SAG (Screen Actors Guild) rules were strictly followed, and Tanya trusted us. In every nude scene, whether it's on a soundstage in Hollywood or on location, you clear the set of people who don't have to be there. That's what we did. As to whether I was there to watch, to tell you the truth, I don't remember. Having seen the scene five hundred times in rushes and a thousand times in the movie, I don't know any more. If I was there, I don't remember!

When the picture was cut, however, the MPAA very much remembered. Since 1968, when Jack Valenti, who then headed the Motion Picture Association of America, revamped Hollywood's strict censorship code into something more realistic and forgiving, studios have demanded that producers deliver a movie with a rating that matches the audience that they hope to attract. *Sheena* was designed as a family film. But when the MPAA's six-person Ratings Board slapped it with an "R" because of Tanya's nudity, we faced a crisis.

The news came in while we were in the final stages of editing at Pinewood studios in London. Not wanting to raise the hackles of the Ratings Board, Columbia wanted to cut the scene. John vigorously objected. It wasn't a sex scene, it was brief, guiltless nudity. He said that his soul would die if he had to cut such sweet moments from his film. That's when someone in Columbia's distribution division came up with a brilliant idea. I only heard about this after the fact, but, rather than send a re-cut version of the film to the Ratings Board in America, they invited the members of the Ratings Board and their families to fly to London to see the film there and work with John to solve the problem. Of course, the week-long trip would be at the expense of the studio, and everyone would stay at the Dorchester Hotel with ample opportunities to sightsee and shop. Apparently the London experience made the film appear different, because *Sheena*'s rating was summarily revised to a family-friendly PG and, in that form, nudity and all, it opened worldwide.

When *Sheena* debuted in the United Kingdom, the British Board of Film Censors cut fourteen seconds to remove, not Tanya's body, but a shot of the mercenary Jorgensen's throat being stabbed with a spear, and another shot of a man on fire. When it was released on home video in 1986, the human violence was restored, but the film got a "15" rating because of a shot of a zebra (horse) being tripped.

What nobody mentioned at the time, but which should be noted now, is that the MPAA made no objection to the many shots of bare-breasted African women in the film's tribal dance sequences. Was it because those women were black? This is akin to the *National Geographic* magazine's decades-long policy of allowing nude photography of women of color but not other races. It's another piece of baggage that *Sheena* carries because of when it was made.[19]

---

19. This hypocrisy was addressed by *NatGeo*'s Editor-in-Chief Susan Goldberg in the magazine's March 12, 2018 edition titled "The Race Issue."

(L-R) Donovan Scott, Tanya Roberts, visiting Kenyan Culture Minister Maina "Jimmy" Wanjigi, me, Ted Wass

(L-R) John Guillermin, Columbia President of Production John Veitch, and me

World Premiere with (L-R) Guy McElwaine, John Guillermin, Henry Plitt, me (Peter C. Borsari photo)

World Premiere with (L-R) Donovan Scott, Guy McElwaine, me. John Guillermin, Henry Plitt (Peter C. Borsari photo)

John Guillermin and me (Peter C. Borsari photo)

Maureen Connell (Mrs. Guillermin), director John Guillermin, and me at the world premiere (Peter C. Borsari photo)

Sheena summons her beast friends

John Guillermin
and I plan a shoot

Me with Associate Producer Christian Ferry who did a great job on the film

African villagers are rousted by an attacking helicopter in the film

Legendary animal trainer Hubert Wells (at left) orders our chimp Caranga to show tricks to visiting members of the Kenyan government

Kenyan Assistant Director Tom Mwangi named his son "Yoram Simba" and sent me their picture

Africa is famous for its acacia trees

Doree Sitterly, one of our animal trainers, provided great care and love to our animals

Academy Award®-winning Director of Photography Pasqualino de Santis and I wait for the sun to come out so we can make a shot

My hair and make-up crew

Here I am enjoying the Kenyan location.

(L-R) Kenyan Culture Minister Maina "Jimmy" Wanjigi, animal trainer Doree Sitterly, and an unidentified Kenyan minister visit our animal compound

(L-R) Hubert Wells, Kenyan Culture Minister Maina "Jimmy" Wanjigi, me, and animal trainer Doree Sitterly in our animal compound. The docile-looking leopard on the ground is the one who later bit off our night watchman's finger

Location, Location, Location

I KEEP STATING HOW TOUGH it was to shoot in Kenya. Rewarding, but tough. The resistance came not at all from the Kenyans but from the land itself. From jungle to savannah, and from flatlands to mountains, the wonderfully varied geography that drew us to Kenya in the first place sometimes worked against us, and this is why everyone who was a part of *Sheena* says it was the roughest film they ever worked on.

The scene in which the Shaman dies in Sheena's arms was one such ordeal. In the story she is rescued from jail and brought to a clearing in the Argenia Forest in Aberdare National Park, nearly four hours north of Nairobi. It wasn't the mileage that posed an obstacle, it was the elevation; the Aberdare Range rises almost 13,000 feet above sea level. We not only had to adjust the carburetors in our vehicles to function in the thinner air, we had to steel ourselves to the lower oxygen levels. Driving up the incline to the very top (naturally that was where John insisted we film the death scene), the roads navigated the steep incline by corkscrewing around the mountain on a one-way passage so narrow that a wrong turn could have plunged any one of us into the gorge below.

Accommodations at the base of the mountain weren't forgiving, either. In those days the Argenia Forest wasn't the tourist site it has since become, and there were not enough rooms available to house all of us. Ted and his family had a room, as did John, and Tanya and her husband Barry. The rest of the crew doubled up. Somehow Donovan Scott's room had not been reserved, so I invited him to share my room.

This is the location where we built a landing strip for a Cessna airplane as well as the place where Vic and Fletch, following Sheena in their Land Rover, are surrounded by lions who are kept at bay when Sheena draws a magic circle around the car for protection. Just to make it safer, she has her pet Rhino stand guard, too. It is also where Sita, our elephant, got sick.

Sita acquitted herself professionally throughout the shoot, but we almost lost her in the cold, wet mountains at 11,000 feet. There was mud during the day and everything froze each night. The animals weren't used to it and, to make it worse, we were all stuck there for three days. Sita began wheezing and one of the trainers diagnosed her with pneumonia. I wanted to get her to a doctor as soon as we could move. Tempers began to rise; some people broke. One of the angry ones teased me, "Is the elephant insured?"

I said, "Yes, for five million dollars."

He said, "Why do you want to send for an elephant doctor? Why don't you let it die and get the insurance and get the fuck out of here because this is an impossible movie to make."

Fortunately, Sita recovered and played a part in one of the best stories of our production.

When the picture wrapped, Sita had to be shipped back to America. This involved loading her into an elephant-sized crate so she could be safely flown on the 747 on which we'd made her travel arrangements. While she was being led up a ramp and into the container, some tourists happened to drive past. They gave no more than a slight glance and sped away. Jules Sylvester, who was in charge of getting Sita home, drove her to the bottom of the hill on the road leading out of the park. By the time he got to the guard station, the guard was laughing so hard that he was crying.

"What's so funny?" Jules asked.

Said the guard, "Did you see some tourists?"

"Yes," Jules said. "They drove past us. Why?"

The guard was still laughing. "They said, 'hurry, quickly, there's a man stealing your elephants.'"

Just when you think you know everything, you realize you don't.

As further indication of how hard it was to be at that location, my friend, logistic manager Danny ben Menahem, told me it was the most uncomfortable he had ever been—and he had been an Israeli commando.

Despite all of these encumbrances, the location was stunningly beautiful. Its beauty was in contrast to the sadness of the Shaman's death scene.

Mystical light, sun through a ground mist. Open on Chango digging a hole with his tusks. Move over solemn-faced Tiki, Marika down on bent forelegs.

> *We find the Shaman lying on a bed of gathered moss, Sheena beside kneeling over her, holding a hand. Sheena's eyes are wet.*

Recalled by Princess Elizabeth of Toro in her memoir, it was not an easy scene to perform. First, she was bridling under the old-age makeup, which demanded that she wake up at 2:00 a.m. for a 3:00 a.m. makeup call and for an 8:00 a.m. shoot, then lie still among the animals and Tanya:

> "Action," John Guillermin called out.
> "Your hand, it is so cold!" was Sheena's opening line.
> "The flame departs," the Shaman answered.
> We had gone halfway through the scene when John Guillermin stopped us. "It is a very strong scene. Tanya, it will not do."
> I understood precisely what Guillermin meant. It wasn't because I was a better actress than Tanya. The difference was, she was acting and I wasn't. Good acting comes from life experience. There were parallels between the Shaman's and my own life. As the Batabe, I held the position of leadership among the Batoro just as the Shaman did among the Zambulis. Right then and there, as the death scene was being played out, the battle not only for my people's survival but for their way of life was raging between the NRM and Obote's fascist forces within Uganda... In the character of the Shaman, I was living out my own experience and crisis... It did not take Tanya

long to summon her acting skills. She adjusted and we shot very good scenes.

Elizabeth is being diplomatic. In truth, although she and the girls playing the young Sheena enjoyed working together, she and Tanya did not have the close relationship that many of the other actors developed. In a way, this was understandable; after all, Tanya was an American actress from New York and Elizabeth was a Princess, a government minister, and a lawyer in Africa. This difference may have caused Elizabeth to think of herself as the star of the film when she was, technically, a supporting player; that is how she was billed in the credits and paid during production (although she was, like all the other featured actors, given first-class travel and accommodations).

It sometimes got testy on the set, but she and Tanya were professionals. They never gave less than one hundred percent (or Guillermin would have seen and corrected it!). It's too bad that there was so much distance between them.

The tension did not go unnoticed. Donovan Scott recalled watching the Shaman's death scene: "It was a tough scene, anyway, because there were like six different animals, maybe more than that, all having to be settled down and taken care of. Then they would start screaming at each other and the animals would get restless. It was a two-minute scene that took about, oh, ten hours."

Contrast this behavior with something I saw on my first job, working with producer-director Otto Preminger on his 1975 film *Rosebud*, which he shot in Israel in 1974. The cast included Peter O'Toole as the hero and Richard

Attenborough as the villain, yet between takes the two of them would sit together discussing British theatre, then come back to the set for their next scene and pretend to be bitter enemies. The only thing Elizabeth and Tanya had in common was their desire to make a good film.

* * *

Two of the more discomfiting scenes in the movie were the bookend cures of injured men in the "healing earth" of Tigora while native dancers (as we now know, the Les Ballets Africains) perform around them. The scenes required, first, a tribesman, and then, at the end, Ted Wass, to be buried up to their necks in the ground. The tribesman wasn't just any tribesman, it was Tom Mwangi, our Kenyan Assistant Director. It was confining and claustrophobic for both of them, but not as bad as it looked. To achieve the effect, we dug a six-foot hole and lowered into it a wood frame box in which they could stand and have some freedom while their head stuck out of the sand. Had it been necessary to escape, they could have been released in a matter of moments. (How they could have scratched an itching nose, however, I'll never know.) It took several hours to shoot each man's scene, and both Ted and Tom didn't complain. In fact, when Tom's wife, who was pregnant at the time, delivered their baby, they named him "Simba Yoram." (I was

Doctor Feelgood

honored, but I wouldn't be a bit surprised if they renamed him after the next producer he worked with.)

THE MEDICINE MAN has a sacred place in tribal civilizations. Anyone who appears to have the secret of Life and Death is celebrated—or later condemned, if the secret doesn't work. Fortunately, science was on our side and we were able to have the services of a competent and clever doctor, Zbigniew Halat, as our company medic. He was a Polish physician who was already ministering to the local tribes on behalf of the United Nations for the munificent sum of $40 a month. From this meager fee he was expected to support a wife and young daughter of perhaps six or seven. It was Christian Ferry who brought this talented man to my attention; in addition to his medical expertise, his young blond-haired, blue-eyed daughter turned out to be a perfect stand-in for Kathryn Gant who played young Sheena. (Kristy Lindsay played the adolescent Sheena.)

When we learned of the pittance he was getting from the U.N., we offered him $400 a month to be our unit doctor and to be on the set at all times in case of sickness or injury. We didn't have to wait long to find him useful. It was a huge company with many actors, extras, and crew members, some of whom visited Florida 2000 and caught a variety of sexually transmitted diseases. We gave the good doctor a new ambulance, a driver, and a nurse, and he was always ready to help.

One morning one of the Samburu tribesmen came to him feeling poorly. Perhaps the man had a cold, perhaps just a headache, but he was clearly under the weather. Dr. Halat gave the man a pill and, within three hours, the man was feeling his old self and telling all his fellow tribesmen what a miracle worker the doctor was. By the next day, Halat had his hands full. The tribe had declared him a magician and from then on over a hundred of them lined up every morning to get one of his "magic" pills. They wouldn't start to work unless he gave them each a pill. Of course, they were just harmless sugar pills, but they had the desired effect. It was if he had performed a psychological miracle: in a twist from *When Harry Met Sally*, it was a placebo version of "I'll have what he's having."

After *Sheena* wrapped, and when his U.N. duties were over, Dr. Halat returned to Poland where the 1980 Solidarity movement under Lech Walesa had reshaped the country and overthrown Communist rule. Halat joined the government as a medical man whose specialty was drinking water; his African experience in this area served him and

Poland well. Years later he invited me to visit him in Warsaw where he promised me a red carpet welcome. When I arrived, however, it was I who had to supply the carpet; when he called for me in a taxi he informed me that he was no longer in the government. I went to the house in Krakow where he was then living with his eighty-year-old father, who was a dentist. His father didn't speak English but shook my hand agreeably and smiled, exposing a mouth full of gold teeth.

Seeing those gold teeth reminded me of what the Nazis did to the Jews in the death camps: they pulled them out of their mouths. While I was still in Poland, I visited the most notorious of those camps, Auschwitz. As I came to the gate, over which were written the words *Arbeit Macht Frei* ("work makes you free"), my hands begin to shake and I shivered all over. I must have run through the camp in ten minutes, passing the cabins where Jews had been confined and died, until I found the crematoria. I remembered that, growing up a kibbutz in Israel that was named after Mordecai Anielewicz, the commander of Jewish resistance in the Warsaw ghetto, many of my fellow kibbutzniks were Holocaust Survivors. I could not help but think of them as I saw the remnants of the hell they had endured at Auschwitz.

I fled the camp to the taxi that was waiting for me with my luggage and ordered the driver to take me to the airport. I took the first plane out of the country, not caring where it was headed. I swore never to come back to Poland.

Heart Attack In the Jungle

It was John Guillermin who brought Lorenzo Semple, Jr. aboard to rewrite the previous screenplay drafts into the final shooting script. The two men had worked together successfully on 1976's *King Kong* and Lorenzo knew the kind of scenes and touches that John liked. He was with us on our second African recce to gather the images and absorb the sensibilities for the actual filming.

An inveterate New Yorker, Lorenzo must have had a shock when he landed in Africa. He constantly discussed the script with John while traveling with us from location to location, adding and changing scenes as the inspiration struck them. We were on safari, living in tents that sometimes were invaded by monkeys, snakes, and other jungle creatures. We had neither lights nor running water; drinking water was supplied. It wasn't the Waldorf-Astoria, let's put it that way.

One evening in Samburu Park it was very dark outside and Lorenzo came to my tent and told me, with an air of discomfort, "Yoram, I think that I am having a heart attack." I didn't know what to do so I told him to go back to his tent while I ran to the tent of the local guide who was the Park gamekeeper, asking him for immediate help. The nearest city was hundreds of miles away and the only way to call for help was on a shortwave radio. The guide told me that the best thing would be to call the Doctors Without Borders center at Wilson Airport. He got them on the line and I spoke to a very nice lady who happened to be a doctor. She asked me to go back to Lorenzo and take his pulse in the ankle and his wrist, which I did. I gave her the result and she asked me some other questions, finally saying that she thought he was having an anxiety attack from fear of the location. (Well, he *was* from New York.) When I asked, "Can you come over now?" she said that we would have to wait till dawn because they don't fly their Cessnas during the night. I went back to Lorenzo and tried to calm him down, advising him to try to go to sleep and that help would soon arrive.

It was six o'clock in the morning and, on the dirt landing strip close to the camp, a small Cessna airplane landed and out of it came the woman I had spoken to. She was, I think, a Canadian doctor who was also a pilot. She went to examine Lorenzo and assured him that he was okay and was not having a heart attack. She was very heroic and looked like Amelia Earhart.

Doctors Without Borders were very likely the only medical help that people living in rural areas could get. Both male and female pilot-doctors served in this remarkable organization. I came to know them very well and had an option to make a movie about them but it turned out not to be practical.

I was afraid Lorenzo would ask to leave and go back to the civilization called "New York" but he relaxed and stayed to continue working with John on the script, making revisions as we shot. In fact, I later learned that he had returned to Kenya with his family to go on a safari where people, when they heard that he had written *Sheena*, were thrilled and complimentary. Not only hadn't he died from a "heart attack," he came to regard *Sheena* as one of the highlights of his career.

"There'd been a script of it already that hadn't worked," he told the Writers Guild Foundation in a 2011 interview when he was 88 years old. "I was called in to rewrite it by John Guillermin, the director, who's a very close friend of mine, still. I love him. *Sheena* [was] a bit controversial. A beautiful white blond girl who—she was a real hot Hollywood cookie—came over and they immediately made her their queen. She could talk to animals and rode a zebra.

"The movie was unbelievably expensive for what it was. Columbia Pictures had made it. Columbia was owned by Coca-Cola at the time and so they had a lot of blocked funds, Coca-Cola money they had in Kenya they couldn't get out because their currency wasn't convertible, so the idea was they'd put the money into the movie and…the profit from the movie would, in effect, launder their money legally and correctly. They didn't care much how much they spent. It was terribly extravagant flying animals over that usually didn't work when they got there anyway.

"Strangely enough," he marveled, "it's one of the few movies I get residuals from."[20]

---

20. Interviewed for "The Writer Speaks" by the Writers Guild Foundation, 2013.

Final Shots

WHEN A FILM COMPANY invades a community they dominate the news. Most people love movies but few people know what it takes to make them. Screenwriter William Goldman put it best when he said, "The most exciting day of your life is your first day on a movie set and the most boring day of your life is your second day on a movie set." I agree; I am quoted on the Internet as saying that one day working on a set is worth more than you can learn in film school. *Watching* a movie is fun; watching a movie get *made* is not.

Sheena hosted its share of local visitors, but not until we left did we discover the goodwill we created that extended to other filmmakers (such as Sydney Pollack who filmed the Oscar®-winning *Out of Africa* there after we left). The *Kenya Times* (which had just editorialized against us over the hotel fight, *q.v.*) reported on April 17 that, "The film and tourism industry share one common goal, and the Minister of Tourism and Wildlife, Mr. Maina "Jimmy" Wanjigi, said yesterday, 'There is a lot in common between the two, we are in the business of providing leisure and knowledge in the society." The article noted local hiring, mentioned Mr. Ferrari, and quoted me as announcing that the film would appear in 17,000 cinemas around the world.

Sheena, which was originally budgeted at $14 million so we could get the green light came in at $20 million, most of which was frozen assets that we couldn't get out of the country anyway. Both Columbia and Coca-Cola were pleased with the results. We screened the film in London for Guy McElwaine and Coca-Cola President Richard C. Gallop, who made the trip especially to see the director's cut, and were happy with it. After the screening they hugged us in excitement and we went to a joyous lunch before they returned to Hollywood. On May 17, 1984, John and I were still in London winding down the production offices when they sent us a cable saying, "Dear John and Yoram: Thanks for a wonderful afternoon. You did a spectacular job and we have a wonderful film. Look forward to seeing you again soon. Regards." With that wind at our backs, we knew the studio would get fully behind the picture.

Opening a movie is as important as making it. When you finally have a product that people can look at, it's very different from when it was words on paper or a vision in a director's head. With millions of dollars suddenly at stake, film companies can't afford to gamble, and over the last hundred years—since the growth and maturity of the studio system—they have honed their marketing skills to the point where the only variable is the film itself.

The business of placing a film in the appropriate theatres at the appropriate time of year is the job of the distribution arm. Enticing the public to see it, however, is the mission of the advertising, marketing, and publicity departments. The man coordinating all these activities for *Sheena* was the brilliant and highly experienced strategist Ashley Boone. Ashley was a rocket. Going to work for United Artists straight after his Brandeis University graduation in 1960, he guided the first James Bond movies to success before being hired away by CBS Films, then Motown Records, then 20th Century-Fox (handling *Star Wars*), before joining Columbia in time to guide *Sheena* into release. While at Fox, he was also, not inconsequentially, the first African-American to head a film company.

Ashley screened *Sheena* and deemed it a children's film, counting on our hard-won PG rating to attract a full range of young people and not just the "kiddie matinee" crowd. His advertising concept (see photo page 76) was to present Tanya in her costume set against the backdrop of the African continent with smaller illustrations depicting animals, hunters, and romance. When John saw this, he raised hell. "This movie is not just for children," he said in the marketing meeting where the sales campaign was presented. "It's for adults as well." This placed Ashley in a tough spot. He had created the campaign based on the film he saw while John wanted a campaign based on the film he felt he made. Moreover, John had the support of studio head Guy McElwaine who had green-lighted the project. "Okay, John," Ashley said, "what's your idea?"

The result can be seen in the display ads (see photo page 79) that hit newspapers and magazines everywhere showing a sparsely-dressed Sheena riding her zebra with the legend of the queen of the jungle written prominently above her beautiful head. The idea was to attract adults, primarily men.

The studio's advertising and marketing departments clicked into high-gear, for they not only had to please the studio, they had to score with Coca-Cola. The studio gave them $9.2 million to spend. A press kit (see appendix C) was sent to hundreds of movie critics and feature editors with "official" information about the film and its production (although nothing—until this book—could possibly describe the challenges we faced and surmounted as a team).

We held the gala world premiere at the Plitt Century Plaza Theatre on the afternoon of August 14 (afternoon was better for the animals who attended). The event was for the benefit of the Wildlife Waystation. Columbia's marketing people brought a taste of Kenya to Los Angeles. Sita the elephant attended, as did Changa the chimp and a troupe of beautifully costumed African dancers. (Before you ask, I wanted to bring Les Ballets Africains to Los Angeles but the cost was prohibitive.) My family joined me. Columbia had blocked off the street for the festivities and decorated the front of the theatre complex to look like Africa. The press was invited and mixed with the American crew and cast members Ted Wass and Donovan Scott (Tanya was off filming the James Bond movie). John Guillermin was there, of course, as was Guy McElwaine and the rest of the studio brass. As the screening ended and the guests moved to a celebratory dinner, I made eye contact with Mace Neufeld, my mentor who had brought me into the American film industry, whom I had proudly invited. He gave me a very strange smile and I didn't know if it was because he loved the movie or because he thought it was ridiculous.

Three days later, *Sheena* opened on 1,200 screens in the U.S.A. and soon followed around the world. It earned a worldwide gross of $5,778,353. This does not include subsequent sales to TV (which was still big in those days) and home video, where it is still available, nor does it reflect fabled Hollywood bookkeeping.

The critics were not as pleased with *Sheena* as the studio was. Typical of the reviewers' reaction was the *Cincinnati Enquirer* who called it simply "the funniest film of the year." Janet Maslin of the *New York Times* went the same way, but expounded, calling it "the perfect summer movie for anyone who's dissatisfied for this season's intentional comedies, and who doesn't believe in looking a gift horse in the mouth. Actually, it's more like a gift zebra." Praising Tanya's physique, Maslin continues, "*Sheena* is less of a love story than a health club movie, since much of it is devoted to ogling the tan and muscular Roberts. She is in very good shape. That, unfortunately, is the best that can be said for her performance. Although the screenplay (by David Newman and Lorenzo Semple, Jr.) leans toward kitschiness, Roberts makes every ill-advised effort to play it straight." Maslin concludes (somewhat confusingly), "*Sheena* isn't the kind of bad movie that makes you wish the filmmakers and players had done things better. They seem to have done exactly as they pleased, and made the right movie for all the wrong reasons."

Sheena even made Siskel & Eberts' list of the worst films of 1984 in their syndicated review show wrap-up. "This is not only a bad movie in its own right," Ebert started, "it doesn't even have the knack of being an old-fashioned good-bad movie like the original Sheena adventures which, at least, you could laugh at." (He must have been referring to the 1955 TV series; there were no earlier Sheena movies.) Picking out Richard Hartley's score, Gene Siskel offered, "You think that was the wrong music? Maybe for a western or something."

"We didn't ask that *Sheena* be a realistic movie," Ebert added, "all we want to know is, is the movie any fun, is it in the tradition of those goofy jungle adventures with big snakes dropping on people. But *Sheena* doesn't even achieve at that level." He also faulted us for not having enough pictures of Tanya standing under a waterfall or sunbathing, but suggested that, had there been more of those, Tanya "could have saved this picture."

Predictably, we practically swept the 1985 Razzie Awards, winning Worst Picture (Paul Aratow, producer, who had little to do with it), Worst Actress (Tanya Roberts), Worst Director (John Guillermin), Worst Screenplay (David Newman and Lorenzo Semple, Jr.), Worst Story (Leslie Stevens), and Worst Musical Score (Richard Hartley). At least they spelled everyone's name right.

Reviews fade, but movies do not. *Sheena* stands as a unique achievement. The critics had no way of knowing—nor should it have mattered to them—the immense challenges we had to face in bringing *Sheena* to the screen. But we knew. We knew that we had succeeded at something that no Hollywood studio had ever attempted with a large-scale dramatic film. That something was Africa.

The experience of making *Sheena* affected everyone connected with her:

- Tanya Roberts continued to appear in a number of feature films including *Inner Sanctum, Legal Tender, Sins of Desire*; to guest in high-profile TV series (*Burke's Law, Silk Stalkings*); voicing "Toni G" in *The Blues Brothers Animated Series*; playing series regular Marge Pinciotti in T*hat 70s Show,* and other episodics. S he had left *That 70s Show* in 2001 to be with her husband, Barry, who was terminally ill, He died in 2006. Tragically, Tanya passed away on January 3, 2021 (as noted in the introduction). She was 65.

- Ted Wass: Although he continued to act in numerous TV series post-*Sheena,* it was while appearing as "Nick Russo" in 130 episodes of *Blossom* that Ted took up directing. Since 1995 he has helmed scores of episodes of such top shows as *Coach, The Jeff Foxworthy Show, Soul Man, Caroline in the City, Two Guys, Two Girls, and Pizza Place, Spin City, The Big Bang Theory,* and *Mom.*

- Donovan Scott: As he did on *Sheena,* "Scotty" has enlivened countless subsequent productions with his comic sensibilities. He has appeared in such varied films and shows as *The Wizard of Speed and Time, Knot's Landing, Back to the Future Part III, Frasier, Blast from the Past, Baby Daddy* and *Days of Our Lives.* He has made a specialty of playing Santa Claus in no fewer than sixteen shows (so far).

- John Guillermin: John directed two more films after *Sheena*: *King Kong Lives*, the sequel to his own *King Kong*, and the TV movie *Dead or Alive*. He was inactive for 27 years before dying on September 27, 2015.

- Pasqualino De Santis: Working primarily on films in his native Italy, Pasqualino De Santis was Director of Photography on Francesco Rosi's *Chronicle of a Death Foretold* and *The Palermo Connection*, the mini-series *Il Commissario Corso*, and *The Colors of the Devil* for Alain Jessua, which was released the year after his death. He is best remembered for his evocative visuals in Franco Zeffirelli's *Romeo and Juliet* (1968, for which he won the Academy Award˚) and Luchino Visconti's *Death in Venice* (1971). He died on June 23, 1996.

- Lorenzo Semple, Jr.: Lorenzo slowed down his writing after the *Sheena* experience. In 1996 he reworked his acclaimed 1968 screenplay for *Pretty Poison* for a TV remake, and saw his original screenplays for *Papillon*, *Three Days of the Condor*, and the *Batman* TV series adapted by others. He died at age 91 on March 28, 2014.

- Frank Price: During the preparation for *Sheena* in 1983, Frank Price had a disagreement with Coca-Cola and left Columbia Pictures to head Universal Studios where he supported *Back to the Future* and *Fletch*, among other hits. He returned to Columbia when Sony purchased the company. At this writing he is 90 and remains one of Hollywood's most respected producers and executives.

- Guy McElwaine: After a rocky tenure at Columbia Pictures (most of the fourteen films he green-lighted flopped, including *Ishtar*), Guy left the studio system to return to agentry at ICM. He stayed there for four years before joining the independent powerhouse Morgan Creek Entertainment in 2002. He died on April 2, 2008.

- Coca-Cola/Columbia: In November 1989, Coca-Cola sold Columbia to Sony. The complex deal included the purchase of a company owned by Peter Guber and Jon Peters, making the two men the heads of Columbia. In 1995 Sony began expanding by acquiring the former MGM studios in Culver City and thoroughly modernizing the facility.

The intervening years have made me think often of *Sheena*, not only as a film but as a statement of where we were as a culture. Like the comic book from which it sprang, it has its origins in a peculiar attitude of Europeans toward any culture that is unlike their own, including African, Hispanic, Polynesian, Original People, and other non-whites. Change has been slow, tumultuous, and ongoing. As I noted earlier, *Sheena* could not be made today, nor should it be. But it was, and looking at it may be the best explanation of why the mechanisms that inspired it are best turned, today, to more constructive purposes.

Appenidx A: A History of Sheena

SHEENA, QUEEN OF THE JUNGLE was born in January 1937 in the first issue of *Wags* magazine from British publisher Joshua B. Power's Fiction House. Her parentage has been disputed. Some historians of the Golden Age of comics credit her to S.M. "Jerry" Iger and Mort Meskin while more sources say that the legendry Will Eisner drew the first entries, after which he left to create his enduring character, The Spirit (1940). Eisner is credited with deriving Sheena's name from the H. Rider Haggard jungle-goddess novel, *She*.

By design, Sheena was a white girl orphaned in the African jungle who learns to communicate with animals and use basic tools so she can deal with such foes as white hunters, slavers, and native Africans. In the story, she is the daughter of Cardwell Rivington, who accompanies her father on an African exploration. When Rivington dies from drinking a witch doctor's magic potion, Sheena is orphaned and raised by the witch doctor who teaches her the ways of the jungle. Later she acquires two friends: Chim, the chimpanzee, and "white hunter" Bob Reynolds (whose last name in subsequent stories is sometimes Rayburn or Reilly).

The parallels with Edgar Rice Burroughs' *Tarzan of the Apes* (1912) are obvious, although it's crucial to note that Burroughs' Tarzan was the cultured Lord Greystoke and not the emblematic illiterate muscleman that Johnny Weissmuller personified in the MGM adventures.

Previous literary works had introduced female jungle heroines in prose stories, but Sheena was the first such character to appear in comic books (predating Wonder Woman by some four years). Although she began in Britain, she made her American debut in 1938 in Fiction House's *Jumbo Comics #1* before earning an eponymous magazine, *Sheena, Queen of the Jungle* in 1942. Her success inspired other publishers, and even her own imprint, Fiction House, to introduce other jungle girl characters.

Things went swingingly until public outcry arose against sex and violence in comic books in the early 1950s fostered by such social critics as Fredric Wertham and Gershon Legman, and coming to a head with the 1954 publication of Wertham's *Seduction of the Innocent*. In that influential book (which Wertham, in his later years, repudiated), comics were blamed for inspiring young readers to a life of rebellion, crime, sex, and other aberrations. Although public ire was directed particularly at violent comics like *Tales from the Crypt*, there was enough disgust left over to criticize comic strip women for their violence, skimpy costumes, and provocative poses. (Seldom noted is that Jumbo Comics, in which Sheena appeared, ceased publication in 1953 long before Wertham's jeremiad was published.)[21]

---

21. Joe Sergei, "Tales From the Code," January 25, 2013 (http://cbldf.org/2013/01/tales-from-the-code-the-near-extinction-of-sheena/)

Sheena made the jump from newsprint to celluloid in 1955 with the syndicated television series *Sheena, Queen of the Jungle* which memorably starred the statuesque model Irish McCalla and Christian Drake as her pal, white hunter Bob Rayburn.[22] The show ran for twenty-five episodes between 1955 and 1956 and carries Will Eisner's and Jerry Iger's names on all twenty-five, although that was a function of creative credit, not actual writing. Fourteen other writers wrote separate episodes.

"I couldn't act, but I could swing through the trees," McCalla told the *Honolulu Advertiser*,[23] doing her own stunts until a vine gave way one day and she fell, breaking her arm. She also wrestled mechanical alligators. After making a handful of guest appearances on adult TV series, she retired and took up painting, becoming an accomplished artist of seascapes and western landscapes and joining Women Artists of the American West. She died in 2002.

Several attempts were made to bring back Sheena in comics, most significantly Blackthorne's *Jungle Comics* and a London Night Studios adaptation of *Sheena* that relocated her to the South American jungle.[24]

Our 1984 production of *Sheena* began with Paul Aratow, Professor of Literature at the University of California,

---

22. There had been a 1935 serial called *Queen of the Jungle*. Its twelve low-budget chapters, which reused footage from the silent 1922 feature *The Jungle Goddess*, had child Joan Lawrence abandoned in Africa while her elders were on a search for radium. She grew up to become a fearsome ruler with native soldiers ready to impose her will on strangers, including her childhood boyfriend who, likewise grown up, sets out to find her and bring her home.

23. "TV actress Irish McCalla dead at 73". Associated Press via *The Honolulu Advertiser*. February 11, 2002. Archived from the original on July 1, 2010.

24. Unsigned, Wikipedia (https://en.wikipedia.org/wiki/Sheena%2C_Queen_of_the_Jungle)

Berkeley. Striking up a friendship with visiting lecturer Will Eisner, Aratow licensed from Eisner the rights to both Sheena and *The Spirit*. (He would produce *The Spirit* as a TV movie in 1987.) A graduate of Cornell and a Fulbright scholar, Aratow's varied career included being the first chef at Alice Waters' celebrated Berkeley restaurant Chez Panisse, and (later) writing episodes for *Beverly Hills Teen, The New Adam 12,* and *Sport Billy*. But all of that came after 1984's *Sheena*.[25]

Paul was nothing if not persistent. After landing the rights, he brought the project to United Artists and Filmways who managed to attach Raquel Welch with Michael Scheff and David Spector writing the script. Financing was coming from an unspecified source in the Far East to the tune of $6 million.[26] The tune changed at the end of 1975 when the project shifted to Universal with Welch still attached but the script now being penned by Robert and Laurie Dillon.[27] By then, Paul was developing the project with David Rinzler (having formed Rinzler-Aratow Productions) and Edward S. Feldman had become attached as Executive Producer. Plans were announced for the picture to roll in early 1976 in South American jungle locations.[28]

It didn't. Instead, it moved over to Avco-Embassy Pictures in mid-1979 where it was assigned a $10 million budget by the studio's Vice President Bob Rehme who said he was holding up production to wait for Cheryl Ladd, Ms.

---

25. Mike Barnes, *The Hollywood Reporter*, January 9, 2016.

26. *Daily Variety*, September 21, 1974

27. *Daily Variety*, December 2, 1975

28. *Variety*, July 29, 1975

Welch having long since departed the project.[29]

At some point Avco-Embassy dropped Sheena and she landed at Columbia who, in April 1980, said that David Newman would write the script for shooting in August in Mexico and then to Kenya in December.[30] At that time, a $7-10 million budget was authorized. Shortly thereafter, the budget was goosed to $10-$15 million and Leslie Stevens was signed to rewrite Newman.

In an April 18, 1983 article for The *Los Angeles Times*, Paul told writer Deborah Caulfield that the August 21 start date for his film was coming eight years, four months, and three turnarounds.[31] Not until December 15 would Sheena actually roll, and it was in Kenya, with the only writer mentioned being Lorenzo Semple, Jr. (*3 Days of the Condor, King Kong, Papillon*).[32]

All told, there were some seventeen versions of the screenplay before Columbia settled on Lorenzo Semple, Jr.'s rewrite (which he and Guillermin revised throughout filming). The final screen credits assign story authorship by David Newman and Leslie Stevens and the screenplay authorship to Newman and Semple.

The film's actual title, by the way, is simply *Sheena*, and that's what appears on screen. The subtitle "Queen of the Jungle" is a legacy of its origins in the comic book.

---

29. *The Hollywood Reporter*, July 22, 1979
30. *Variety*, April 20, 1980
31. *Los Angeles Times*, April 18, 1983
32. *Variety*, December 21, 1983

Appenidx B: Film Synopsis

PHILIP AND BETSY AMES are medical anthropologists from the Philadelphia Medical Mission whose fascination with the "healing earth" ceremony of the Zambuli tribe has brought them to the sacred Gudjara Mountains of Africa. They witness a ceremony at which tribal dancers whirl around a sick man buried up to his head in the ground and are amazed when he is withdrawn from the sand cured of whatever malady had brought on the treatment. Returning to the scene of the ceremony the next day to take samples of the healing earth, the Ames are killed in a cave-in, orphaning their young daughter, Janet. The whole event has been watched by a Zambuli Shaman (the term *witch doctor* being considered offensive) who believes that the child has been saved from death by grace of the mountains. She believes the child to be a god and adopts her, appointing herself guardian, and renaming Janet "Sheena."

SHAMAN: "The prophesy has come to pass. On a day when the sacred mountain cries out, a golden girl-child will come from the depths of Gudjaral, and she shall grow in wisdom and be the protector of the Zambuli and all their creatures. And she shall be called by the name of Sheena, Queen of the jungle."

As Sheena grows into a dynamic and attractive blond woman, the Shaman teaches her how to psychically bond with the animals and become their protector. Fortunately, the country of Tigora in which they dwell is also protected by a benign ruler, King Jabalani, who protects his nation's resources by outlawing foreign developers.

King Jabalani's younger brother, Prince Otwani, however, opposes this policy and conspires with Jabalani's fiancée, Countess Zanda, to assassinate the King. The Shaman has a vision that tragedy is about to befall the monarch and journeys to Tigora's capitol, Azan, to warn him. She arrives in the city only to be arrested by corrupt policemen who jail her rather than pass along her warnings.

Enter now American TV sports reporter Vic Casey who is a friend of Prince Otwani, having gone to school with him where the Prince was a college football star. Casey and his partner, Fletch Agronsky, have come to Tigora to shoot a TV sports documentary about Otwani. As their plane descends to the airport, Fletch sees a blond woman riding a zebra, but Vic insists his friend must be hallucinating.

Vic and Fletch begin shooting their TV feature on King Jabalani by shooting at a State dinner. The Shaman tries crashing the dinner to warn Jabalani for his safety, but is detained; when he is killed anyway, the Shaman is arrested for it. Vic and Fletch caught the killing on camera and, when Fletch sees it and realizes that the Shaman is innocent, he has to get it out of the country and rush the footage to the network for broadcast. But first they must interview the Shaman, who has been put into a local jail. As they arrive at the jail, they are interrupted by Chango the elephant, working under Sheena's command, who literally pulls the flimsy building apart to free the Shaman. Other animals (Marika the zebra and Tiki the chimp) rush in to help, and Sheena carries the Shaman, who has been beaten, into the jungle as Vic and Fletch race after them.

Vic's schoolmate Prince Otwani assumes the mantle of King and orders his Black Beret Colonel Jorgensen and his mercenaries to find Sheena and kill the Shaman before she talks. He also wants Sheena, and so does Zanda, but out of jealousy. It develops that Otwani's scheme is to kill the people of the Zambuli tribe, take their land, and open it to strip mining for its valuable titanium.

Vic and Fletch do, indeed, meet Sheena when their Land Rover is surrounded by lions and she swings down to them asking, "Do you want to die?" demanding that they go back and tell other men not to kill her tribe. Vic explains that he's the one who stopped the guards from killing her, and Sheena draws a safe circle around the Land Rover to protect them from animals while she rides off to be with the Shaman. Tibor the lion stands guard to make sure.

Sheena finds the Shaman, who dies in her arms, telling her to guard the land from men who would defile it.

Meanwhile, Fletch is unable to ship the film to the network; Otwani has closed the airports.

Jorgensen's mercenaries find Sheena and Vic, who narrowly escape by hiding behind a tree. Later they sleep in the jungle and, next day, start falling in love even as they are pursued by Jorgensen and Otwani. When their followers get close, Sheena telepathically commands her elephant Chango to topple a huge tree on the road, blocking them. The mercenaries blow the road clear with dynamite and proceed into Zambuli territory, slaughtering the tribes people. Sheena and Vic helplessly witness this massacre from afar. Vic vows to bring Sheena to the city where they can report this atrocity to the authorities. They start by firebombing a convoy, but the flames are blown out by Otwani's gunship copter. As strategy, they surrender to Otwani. Zanda wants to throw Sheena into the Zambuli falls, but Otwani summons Vic. The two old friends are now sworn enemies. Vic tells Otwani that he has the incriminating footage and offers him a trade for a treaty that will bring peace to the Zambuli. Otwani agrees but then tells Jorgensen to kill Vic. Vic escapes his captors and drives their Land Rover off to find Sheena.

Sheena is aloft with Zanda, but when Zanda and her pilot try to drop Sheena into the falls, Sheena summons a flock of flamingos who attack the helicopter and cause it to crash. Sheena escapes to gather the Zambuli to join her in fighting Otwani's mercenaries. This they do in a pitched jungle battle where Otwani is the only one to make it out alive.

On the Serengeti, Sheena shoots her arrow into Otwani's heart, fulfilling the Shaman's prophesy, but stands in the deadly path of Otwani's car. Vic crashes his car into the oncoming vehicle but is badly burned. Sheena uses the healing earth ceremony to save Vic's life.

Vic takes a sample of the healing earth to America to analyze as a cure for disease. He tells Sheena that he loves her but cannot stay with her or bring her back with him. He warns that other men may come to destroy her world, but he wants to leave her in peace in the jungle. She records an audiotape farewell message that he plays back to himself as he and Fletch head home.

Appenidx C: Presskit

NOW THAT YOU'VE READ *my personal memories of making* Sheena, *it may be interesting to you to see what Columbia Pictures released to the press in advance of the picture's opening. This Press kit follows the studio format for titles and punctuation.*

"SHEENA"
Production Information

A young American girl is orphaned when she is separated from her parents in the depths of the African forest. She is found and adopted by a tribal Shaman who recognizes her as the fulfillment of an ancient prophecy and names her 'Sheena, Queen of the Jungle.' Growing up according to the laws of nature, Sheena strikes a civilized harmony with the animal kingdom over which she presides. Years pass and the child blossoms into a beautiful woman.

From New York City, a wisecracking television sports program producer travels to Africa for a story on a royal football player. His assignment unexpectedly embroils him in a world of vicious political intrigue and brings him face to face with Sheena.

Action, adventure and romance unfold in this tiny, colorful nation as modern warfare and ideologies threaten an idyllic way of life. At the same time, a unique love story emerges between an urbane man-of-the-world and a beautiful, primeval woman.

Columbia Pictures presents a John Guillermin Film, "Sheena," directed by John Guillermin and starring Tanya Roberts, Ted Wass, and Donovan Scott. David Newman and Lorenzo Semple, Jr. wrote the screenplay from a story by Newman and Leslie Stevens. Paul Aratow produced and Yoram Ben-Ami is Executive Producer.

About the Production...

"Sheena" is a spectacular romantic adventure story set against a backdrop of the lush equatorial forests, snow-peaked mountains and rolling plains of Africa. Filmed entirely on location in Kenya, "Sheena" had its origins in the popular comic strip first published in the U.S. in 1938 which later became a television series.

According to executive producer Yoram Ben-Ami, "Sheena" was a complicated production from a logistical standpoint. "People always tell you to shoot pictures at simple locations and never use animals! We broke both rules."

In a breaking those rules, however, director John Guillermin and his crew wound up with spectacular locations and a unique film experience. "We spent about two years in preproduction looking for locations and for ways to shoot the picture. We did not want to go into the studio and I think that decision was sound as far as this film is concerned. We are telling a story which has many elements of fantasy, and authentic settings are invaluable in helping convince an audience."

For Guillermin, "the feel of the finished product is very important. There should be no way to get that 'feel' except by working and living in Africa. All of us, Tanya, Ted, the rest of the cast and crew, fell to the imprint of Africa as we were shooting. That reaction made the story come to life."

Taking an entire production crew comprised of several different nationalities to a location as vast and inaccessible as Africa is no small achievement. Executive producer Ben-Ami remarked, "In Hollywood, if you need an actor, prop or piece of equipment, all you do is make a phone call. In Kenya, it sometimes took two days to get to a phone."

Another problem the filmmakers faced was the length of time it took to get the dailies back from London, which was the closest place to have the film processed. It took two weeks before the dailies arrived back in Africa and by that time the crew would have moved on to another location. Guillermin and crew had to hope that everything they shot was right the first time around.

Moving from place to place was difficult, at best. "The locations we used were all quite far from one another and involved big moves each time," says Ben-Ami. "We were very lucky to be able to move from place to place without losing too much time, which is key because time is money."

One thing that helped ease the problems of shooting in such a vast location was the use of three film crews. They all worked simultaneously, with Guillermin and Ben-Ami moving from one location to the next to coordinate what amounted to three different phases of production happening all at once.

Logistics were further complicated by the problem of communication among a cast and crew consisting of people from several different countries. There were at least 28 different languages on the set at any given time, with people from 14 different countries and groups of African natives, each with its own distinct dialect.

The film's schedule was long and demanding—four and a half months of shooting in various regions of Africa with climactic variations, and the added hazard of trying to fit an 18-week schedule into a 12-week season.

"Incoming crew should be informed that they should have clothing to protect them against heat and dust, sun and fast eroding laundry services," read a telex from Nairobi headquarters. Several times throughout production, a punishing equatorial sun heated the set to temperatures which reached 120° F by 10:00 a.m.

One of the key elements in the filming of "Sheena" was the use of animals. Veteran animal trainer Hubert Wells was responsible for making sure the animals performed according to the needs of the script, as well as ensuring the safety of the cast and crew working with these animals.

Several trained animals were flown to Kenya from Hollywood and it was important to see that the trained animals were not harmed by those which roamed wild around the set. According to Wells, "We flew over an elephant, a rhino, five lions, four leopards, four chimpanzees, five horses and

16 birds. It was probably the largest shipment of animals back to Africa for a film, and just getting all the necessary permits to bring them in and out of the country was a superhuman test."

Despite the difficulties encountered during production on "Sheena," everyone connected with the film agrees the end result was worth the time and effort.

"It was the hardest film I've ever worked on," says Tanya Roberts, "but at the same time the most gratifying. It was so amazingly beautiful in Africa—the wildlife, the sunrises and sunsets, the skies, the land and the people."

Guillermin adds, "This country (Africa) is harsh but magnificent. The people are proud but helpful. The Kenyan government went out of its way to help us, and, of course, the wildlife is the greatest remaining living heritage still left on this earth."

Reflecting on the production, "Sheena" executive producer Yoram Ben-Ami comments, "to be perfectly honest, it's like fighting for something and winning. The film looks great—the scenery is beautiful, the acting is beautiful and the locations look incredible."

Producer Paul Aratow describes "Sheena" as an action-adventure-fantasy piece with a beautiful, exotic setting. It's also kind of fun and sexy, and those are all attractive elements. Sheena is a character who represents positive things. She cares about the land, the animals and her fellow man."

About the Cast...

TANYA ROBERTS is Sheena. She has a rare combination of natural beauty and raw energy that brings the character to life on screen. Even on paper, the Sheena character was so compelling that Miss Roberts decided when she read the script that she simply had to play that role.

"When I read the script, I just freaked—it was so great," the actress recalled. "It's really a terrific part, romantic yet full of adventure. Sheena is a wonderful person and her world is very special."

Winning the role of Sheena was only the beginning for Miss Roberts, who had to transform herself into the character. Wholly committed to the role, the striking brunette bleached her hair blond. Next she experimented with several different accents and came up with the one she felt suited Sheena. Then came the hard part: nearly a year-long period of intensive physical training, a routine she has continued in order to maintain her perfect physique.

Probably best known for her portrayal of Julie Rogers during the fifth season of ABC's hit series, "*Charlie's Angels*," the New York-born actress began her career at age 17 doing national commercials. During this time she appeared Off-Broadway in productions "*Picnic*," "*Antigone*" and "*Liliom*," and also found time to study at the Herbert Berghof Studios under Uta Hagen, as well as with Alice Spivac, Alice Hermes and the venerable Lee Strasberg and at the Canadian Academy under John Winslow.

At 18 she married up-and-coming young writer Barry Roberts and the two spent the next five years trying to make their way in New York before going to Hollywood in 1977.

After a pair of television movies, "Pleasure Cove" and "Zuma Beach," and three theatrical films, "California Dreaming," "Tourist Trap" "Racquet," Miss Roberts was cast with Michelle Phillips in a special two-hour segment of Aaron Spelling's "Vega$," in which Spelling, impressed with what he saw, mentally placed her on the front burner for his "Charlie's Angels" search.

Landing the "Charlie's Angels" role catapulted Miss Roberts to stardom. Following the end of that enormously successful series, this particular angel moved straight into motion pictures with her starring role as Kiri, the medieval princess, in the 1982 feature film, "Beastmaster."

Most recently, Miss Roberts starred with Stacy Keach in the successful CBS-TV movie, "Mickey Spillane's Mike Hammer 'Murder Me, Murder You.'"

TED WASS is Vic Casey, the wisecracking TV journalist who goes to Africa to scoop a story and is, instead, captivated by Sheena.

Prior to his co starring role in "Sheena," Wass spent most of his acting career in comedies, most of which were filmed in the comfortable confines of studio lots. With the role of Vic Casey, he was forced to spend some seven months on location in Africa—not quite a typical backlot set!

The Ohio-born Wass moved to Los Angeles in 1977 to pursue a film career. Within three months he had landed a guest-starring role in "Family" and later was cast as Danny Dallas in "Soap."

Prior to finishing "Soap," Wass replaced Tony Roberts in the musical "They're Playing Our Song" on Broadway during the summer of 1981. While he was in New York, Wass was chosen by Director Blake Edwards to star in "The

Curse of the Pink Panther" as Clifford Sleigh, a role that was created to fill the gap caused by Peter Sellers' death. Wass recently starred with George Burns in the soon-to-be-released, "Oh, God! You Devil."

Comedy actor DONOVAN SCOTT plays Fletch Agronsky, the archetypal city dweller who finds himself in the sticky situation in deepest, darkest Africa. Scott's first love had always been the theater, but he decided to go to Los Angeles and try his luck in film. He promptly found himself back on the stage in a rock musical called "Zen Boogie," but his first feature film role followed shortly thereafter when he co-starred with Robin Williams in "Popeye." Scott has also appeared in "Zorro, the Gay Blade," "Savannah Smiles" and the recent comedy hit "Police Academy."

The Shaman is played by the real-life PRINCESS ELIZABETH OF TORO. Elizabeth was born into the Royal Court of Toro, at that time in independent state but now incorporated into present-day Uganda. Educated at Cambridge and admitted to the English bar in 1965, the stunning Princess began receiving modeling offers that were too good to pass up. Leaving law for a successful career as a high fashion model, Elizabeth quickly became an international jet-setter, but was drawn back to her roots in Uganda when, at the request of President Idi Amin, she became Minister of Foreign Affairs. Her diplomatic career ended, however, when she refused Amin's proposal of marriage and she took exile in Kenya. "Sheena" is her first major film.

Martinique-born FRANCE ZOBDA plays the evil Princess Zanda. Miss Zobda's acting career began with French film director Christian Lara's film "Adieu Foulards," in which she played the female lead which was written specifically for her. Miss Zobda was cast in "Sheena" after a Paris agent recommended her to director Guillermin.

Ruthless Prince Otwani is played by Jamaican-born TREVOR THOMAS. Brought up and educated in England, Thomas started his career assisting an advertising photographer until he decided life was more interesting on the other side of the camera. His first leading role on television was in Thames TV's "The Road Runner," which was followed by "Hole in Babylon" for the BBC and "Murder at the Wedding." He has guest-starred in the British series "Minder," "The Professionals," and "Return of the Saint." His first film was "Los Adolescents" with Anthony Andrews and Koo Stark, followed by "Black Joy," "Inseminoid" and "Yesterday's Hero." He has worked extensively on the London stage, most recently in a production of "The Passion" at the National Theatre.

CLIFTON JONES, who plays King Jabalani, has appeared on the London stage in productions of "Billy Budd," "Moon on a Rainbow Stage" and "A Taste of Honey," as well as British television productions of "The Raid," "Anything You Say," "The Troubleshooters," "Space 1999," "The Professionals" and the upcoming BBC series "All the World's a Stage."

Completing the cast are SYLVESTER WILLIAMS as Juke, ERROL JOHN as Bolu and JOHN FORGEHAN as Jorgenson. KATHRYN GANT is Janet Ames the young Sheena.

About the Filmmakers...

French-Born JOHN GUILLERMIN began his career as a documentary filmmaker following service with the RAF during World War II. He spent time in Hollywood observing feature production and returned to Britain to write two screenplays and then made his debut as a feature film director. Guillermin includes in the compendium of films such hits as "The Blue Max," "The Towering Inferno," the 1976 remake of "King Kong" and Agatha Christie's "Death on the Nile."

Executive Producer YORAM BEN-AMI began his film career as an assistant director and worked his way up to production manager of films produced in his native Israel, as well as on various locations throughout Western Europe. He most recently produced the American film "Lone Wolf McQuade."

Nearly 10 years ago, the first-time producer PAUL ARATOW came to Hollywood with a dream and a list of possible film projects, among them "Sheena." After several script rewrites and commitments from different studios, Aratow's dream of "Sheena" is finally a reality. "The trick to getting a project like this off the ground," he says, "is to hang in there until you get enough people on your side. If you're lucky to get the support you need, you simply go out and hire the best people you can. Then you pray..."

Screenwriters DAVID NEWMAN and LORENZO SEMPLE, JR. have between them some impressive screen credits. Newman has written "Superman" and "Superman II," "Bad Company," "What's Up, Doc?," "There Was a Crooked Man" and "Still of the Night." Semple includes among his credits "Papillon," "The Parallax View," "Three Days of the Condor," "The Drowning Pool" and the 1976 remake of "King Kong."

Italian master cinematographer PASQUALINO De SANTIS won an Oscar® for his work on Zeffirelli's "Romeo and Juliet" and includes among his credits "Death in Venice," "The Conversation Piece," "The Innocent" and "A Special Day."

British-born editor RAY LOVEJOY was the assistant editor on "Dr. Strangelove" and "Lawrence of Arabia" before becoming an editor on Stanley Kubrick's classic "2001: A Space Odyssey." His other films include "A Day in the Death of Joe Egg," "The Ruling Class" and, again with Kubrick, "The Shining." Most recently, Lovejoy was the editor of the Oscar®-nominated film, "The Dresser," which starred Albert Finney and Tom Courtenay.

The musical score for "Sheena" is by RICHARD HARTLEY, whose credits include several scores for British features, among them "The Rocky Horror Picture Show."

Columbia Pictures present a John Guillermin Film, "Sheena," starring Tanya Roberts, Ted Wass and Donovan Scott, and directed by John Guillermin. David Newman and Lorenzo Semple, Jr. wrote the screenplay from a story by Newman and Leslie Stevens. Paul Aratow produced and Yoram Ben-Ami is executive producer.

Tanya Roberts stars as "SHEENA," a beautiful primeval woman who possesses a magical gift and must fight to save her idyllic world [in Columbia Pictures' romantic adventure directed by John Guillermin and co-starring ted Wass and Donovan Scott. David Newman and Lorenzo Semple, Jr. wrote the screenplay based on a story by Newman and Leslie Stevens. Paul Aratow produced and Yoram Ben-Ami is executive producer.]

Tanya Roberts and Ted Wass are thrown together in a world where political unrest threatens a beautiful woman and her jungle paradise.

Tanya Roberts defiantly displays the bonds against which she must fight to protect her people.

Donovan Scott becomes the unwilling subject of a lion's affections.

Tanya Roberts comforts aging tribal Shaman, Princess Elizabeth of Toro, as the beautiful and gifted young woman assumes her mystical role as the jungle queen.

Tanya Roberts stars in Columbia Pictures' "SHEENA," a romantic adventure in which a beautiful and gifted primeval woman must fight to protect her idyllic world from outside forces.

Princess Elizabeth of Toro looks on as the evil Trevor Thomas gives an order determining her fate.

Tanya Roberts and Ted Wass fall in love against tremendous odds when modern politics threaten a tiny, third-world nation.

Tanya Roberts battles to save her jungle kingdom when a vicious political coup threatens to destroy her peaceful world.

Director John Guillermin on the set of his Columbia Pictures "SHEENA."

Index

A

Aberdare Park 54, 64, 114, 115, 129
advertising campaigns 76, 145, 146, 173
Africa 2-5, 7, 8, 11-15, 19, 26, 27, 32, 36-39, 44, 46, 47, 51-53, 55, 57, 59, 61, 73, 89, 93, 99-101, 108, 109, 114, 125-127, 133, 139, 143, 146, 148, 155, 159, 165-169, 171, 172
Agronsky, Fletcher "Fletch" 36, 37, 64, 77, 105, 130, 150, 160, 161, 163, 172
Allen, Tor 26, 27
Ames, Philip and Betsy
Amin, Idi 35, 36, 94, 172
Anielewicz, Mordechai 137
"Animal Annie" Olivecrona (see Olivecrona)
Aratow, Paul 39, 40, 135, 148, 156, 166, 169, 174, 176, 177
Argenia Forest 64, 129, 130
Attenborough, Richard 133
auditioning performers 13, 33, 35-37, 46, 90, 97

B

Ballets Africains, Les 90-93, 98, 134, 146
Baryshnikov, Mikhail 90

Beastmaster, The 46, 171
below-the-line (definition) 5
Ben-ami, Ani 8, 33
Ben-ami, Yoram 4, 5, 10, 15, 34, 41, 51, 83, 85, 94, 100, 106, 124, 134, 139, 144, 166, 169, 174, 176, 177
Benami, Dory 8, 20, 25, 71
Blackthorne's *Jungle Comics* 155
blocked funds 4. 12. 39, 66, 103, 104, 141, 144, 146 frozen assets
Blossom 50, 149
Blum, Victoria Leigh (see Tanya Roberts) 44
Bogart, Humphrey 26
Boniface 68
Boone, Ashley 145
Broccoli, Albert R. "Cubby" 47
budget 4, 6, 12, 29-32, 84, 104, 105, 111, 144, 156, 157
Burroughs, Edgar Rice 154

C

Caranga 52, 58, 59, 124
Carrera, Barbara 5
Carradine, David 5
Cartier, Maggie 33, 34
Casablanca 15
Casey, Vic 49, 55, 64, 90, 115, 160-161, 163, 171

censors 116, 117
Charlie's Angels 1, 44-46, 170, 171
chimps 43, 52, 53, 58-60, 80, 82, 115, 124, 146, 153, 161, 168
Clayton, Patrick 41
Coca-Cola 4, 7, 12, 13, 18, 19, 27, 29, 38-40, 78, 103, 104, 141, 144, 146, 150, 151
Colgems Productions 34, 102, 104
Colonel Jorgensen 161
Columbia ix, 1-4, 5-8, 13, 15, 18, 27, 29, 30, 32-34, 39, 40, 43-44, 46, 49, 90, 93, 97, 98, 102-103, 116, 119, 141, 144-146, 150, 151, 157, 165, 166, 176, 177, 181, 183
Conakry, Guinea 91, 94
Connell, Maureen 121

D

Dallas, Danny 49, 171
De Santis, Pasqualino 38, 55, 126, 150, 175
Dickey, James 11
Dillon, Robert and Laurie 156
Doctor Dolittle 69
Dorchester Hotel 33, 34, 117
Drake, Christian 155

E

Earhart, Amelia 140
Ebert, Roger 147, 148
Edwards, Blake 171
Eisner, Will 2, 153, 155, 156
elephants 27, 33, 43, 52-56, 57, 74, 83, 84, 130, 131, 146, 161, 162, 168
Elizabeth of Toro 35, 36, 60, 78, 132, 133, 172, 180, 181
Embakasi Airport 13

F

Fairmont Hotels 14
fed 52, 54, 108
Feinberg, Jane 33
Feldman, Edward S. 156
Ferrari, Pierre 13, 14, 16, 144
Ferry, Christian 39, 85, 86, 105, 123, 135
flamingos 52, 53, 69-71, 162
Florida 2000 17, 108, 136
Forgeham, John 35, 174

G

Gant, Kathryn 174
Gil, Miguel 38, 41
Goldman, William 143
Greystoke, Lord (Tarzan) 154
Guber, Peter 151
Gudjara 112, 113, 159
Guillermin, John 1, 3, 6-9, 13, 19, 25, 27, 31-33, 36-38, 40, 41, 44, 49, 52, 58, 63, 66, 76, 78, 79, 81, 90, 95, 96, 107, 110, 119-122, 132, 133, 139, 141, 146, 148, 150, 157, 166-169, 173, 174, 176, 177, 183
Guillermin, Michael 83-84, 86
Guinea 90-94, 97, 98

H

Hagen, Uta 45, 170
Haggard, H. Rider 153
Halat, Dr. Zbigniew 135, 136
Hartley Richard 86, 91, 92, 89, 148, 175
Hatari 61
Heifetz, Jascha 22
Heston, Charlton 11

I

Iger, Jerry 2, 153, 155
Israel 2, 4, 15, 16, 19, 20, 21, 33, 34, 99, 107, 131, 133, 137, 174

J

Jabalani, Prince 35, 56, 82, 160, 173
Jones, Clifton 35, 82, 94, 173
Jorgensen 35, 161, 162
Julienne, Rémy 38

K

Kenya 4, 8, 9, 10-13, 15, 17, 19, 21, 23, 25, 26, 27, 29, 31, 38, 43, 46, 50, 52-54, 58, 60, 61, 69, 70, 72, 73, 83, 90, 91, 93, 98, 99, 101-106, 107-108, 114, 119, 124, 128, 129, 134, 141, 143, 146, 157, 166-169, 172
Kenyatta, Jomo 12, 13
Kikuyu tribe 11, 11, 114
Kipling, Rudyard x
Kleven, Max 52, 84

L

Lake Naivasha 57, 112
Lake Nakuru 70
Leary, Dr. Timothy 47
Lindsay. Kristy 135
lions 8, 13, 43, 51, 53, 54, 63-69, 71, 73, 74, 99, 114, 126, 127, 148, 150, 161, 166, 168, 180
Lovejoy, Ray 110, 175

M

Maasai 42, 73, 74, 103, 104, 114
Margolin, Janet 49
Marika 52, 57, 131, 161

Martin, Steve 69, 90, 110
Marx, Michael 34
McCalla, Irish 155
McElwaine, Guy 1, 6, 7. 19, 27, 32, 37, 40, 46, 50, 53, 56, 83, 84, 86, 110, 111, 120, 144-146, 151
Menahem, Dany Ben 131
Meskin, Mort 153
Moi, Daniel arap 8, 13, 14, 53, 58, 105
Morricone, Ennio 2
MPAA 116, 117
Mr. X 15, 16, 19
Murton, Gary 39, 90, 110, 111
Musamba, General 105
Mwangi, Tom 110, 124, 134
mzungu 17, 18

N

Nairobi, Kenya 13, 14, 18, 38, 49, 58, 70, 83, 85, 86, 90, 94, 95, 97, 101, 105, 111, 112, 129, 168
Ness Ziona 21, 23
Neufeld, Mace 146
Norfolk Hotel 14, 25, 38, 50, 85, 101, 102
Norris, Chuck 5
Nyabongo, Elizabeth (Princess Elizabeth of Toro) 36

O

Obama, Barack xi
O'Brien, Lance ix
Olivecrona, "Animal Annie" 69
Olroyd, Susi 10
Otwani, Prince 34, 37, 57, 82, 160-162, 173
O'Toole, Peter 133

P

Patrick 41, 42
Paul 39, 40, 98, 148, 155-157, 166, 169, 174, 176, 177

Pepsi-Cola 7
Peters, Jon 151
Pingel, Mike ix
Pollack, Sydney 143
Popeye 172
Power, Joshua 153
Preminger, Otto 33, 133
Price, Frank 8, 24, 30, 32, 46, 150

R

Racial issues x, 38, 100-102, 117, 161
RAF 9, 41, 174
recce 8, 13, 17, 19, 31, 38-41, 112, 139
Rehme, Bob 156
Reilly, Bob (also Reynolds) 153
Reynolds, Sled 61, 69, 72
rhinos 52, 54, 60, 61, 67, 68, 73, 112, 130, 168
Rinzler, David 156
Rivington, Cardwell 153
Roberts, Barry 44, 45, 47, 130, 149, 170
Roberts, Tanya ix, 1, 3, 20, 43-47, 50, 55, 65, 72, 75, 78, 80-82, 114-117, 119, 130, 132,133, 145-149, 166, 167, 169-171, 176-182
Rosebud 33, 133
Rukidi III of Toro 36
Russo, Nick 149

S

Samburu 103, 114, 136, 139
"Sandy" (pseudonym) 94
Schwartz 2-5, 7, 13
Scott, Donovan "Scotty" 37, 50, 60, 64-67, 77, 87, 119, 120, 133, 146, 149, 166, 172, 176, 177, 180
Semple, Lorenzo, Jr. 17, 39, 71, 139-141, 147, 148, 150, 157, 166, 175-177
Sheena 1-4, 6, 8, 10-14, 16, 18, 20, 22, 24, 26, 29, 30, 32, 34-36, 38-40, 42-44, 46, 47, 49-52, 54-58, 60, 63-68, 70-72, 74, 76, 78, 80-84, 86, 89-92, 94, 96, 98-100, 102, 104, 106, 108, 110, 112-117, 120, 122, 124, 126, 128-130, 132, 134-136, 140, 141, 143-151, 153-157, 159-163, 165, 166, 168-178, 180-183, 186
Shrager, Sheldon "Shel" 2, 5, 6, 27, 45, 46.110, 111
Sindiyo, Daniel 53, 54, 107
Siskel, Gene 147, 148
Smight, Jack 11
Sony Pictures 150, 151
Spelling, Aaron 171
Stefanovich, Ed 103
Stevens, Leslie 2, 148, 157, 166, 176, 177
Strasberg, Lee 45, 170
Swahili 1-3, 5, 7, 8, 14, 17, 56
Sylvester, Jules 44, 58, 68, 69, 72, 73, 80, 131, 174

T

Tarzan 11, 12, 37, 154
Thomas, Trevor 34, 82, 173, 181
Thompson Falls 71,72
Tigora 36, 56, 160
Touré, Ahmed Sekou 91
trainers 44, 52, 54, 56, 61, 63, 69, 72, 124, 125, 130, 168

U

Uganda 35, 36, 46, 132, 172
Unions 12

V

Valenti, Jack 116
Veitch, John 2, 6, 7, 119
Visconti, Luchino 150

W

Walesa, Lech 136
Wanjigi, Maina "Jimmy" 119, 128, 143
Ward-Booth 70, 100
Wass, Julian
Wass, Matilda 50
Wass, Ted 49, 50, 55, 60, 64, 66-68, 82, 115, 119, 130, 134, 146, 149, 166, 167, 171, 172, 176-178, 182
Weissmuller. Johnny 37, 154
Welch , Raquel 156, 157
Wells, Hubert 51, 52, 58-61, 63, 64, 66, 68, 69, 124, 128, 168
Wertham, Dr. Frederic 154
Wilberforce, Price (Nyabongo) 36
Wilson Airport 140
Wolper, David L. 10

Y

Yambo, Joe S. 103

Z

Zambo, Italo 91
Zambuli 70, 89, 113, 114, 132, 159-162
Zanda, Countess 35, 71, 82, 160-162, 173
Zanuck, Darryl F. 9
Zobda , France 35, 82, 173

www.ingramcontent.com/pod-product-compliance
Lightning Source LLC
Chambersburg PA
CBHW051054160426
43193CB00010B/1182